GHOSTS

GHOSTS

**AN EXPLORATION OF THE SPIRIT WORLD,
FROM APPARITIONS TO HAUNTED PLACES**

Paul Roland

This edition published in 2012 by Arcturus Publishing Limited
26/27 Bickels Yard, 151–153 Bermondsey Street,
London SE1 3HA

AD002445EN

Printed in the UK

Contents

12 Introduction

19 Chapter 1 – Belief in the soul

22 Cults of the dead

26 Sacred spirits

31 Spirits in the Scriptures

35 Ancient apparitions

38 Restless spirits

43 Chapter 2 – The night side of nature

46 Willington Mill

51 The Fox sisters

57 The birth of spiritualism

60 A surplus of spirits

65 The haunting of Charles Dickens

68 Ghost lights

71 The ghost club

74 A ghostly intruder

CONTENTS

76 Concern from beyond the grave

77 Suicide sighting

80 Last will and testament

83 A dispiriting response

85 Time delayed proof

87 Frauds and fakes

90 Spectral soldiers

95 A 'strange meeting'

98 The conversion of Conan Doyle

103 The phantom fayre

105 Mass materializations

109 Chapter 3 – Living apparitions

112 The stone tape theory

113 In two places at once

117 The absent MP

117 Phantom forerunners

120 Getting ahead of themselves

122 Thought forms

125 Crisis apparitions

128 Escaping worldly bonds

132 A ghost in the mirror

136 Projecting his own ghost

138 Inducing an out-of-body experience

141 The astral visit

142 A message from the other side

145 The psychologist and the spirit

150 Psychology and the paranormal

155 The haunted cottage

158 Out of this world

162 Crisis of faith

165 Voices from beyond

168 Recording EVP

169 The Pope's parapsychologists

177 Chapter 4 – Talking to the dead

179 Science and the spirit world

181 Our sixth sense

185 Convincing evidence

186 Positive benefits

192 Betty Shine

196 The psychic cleric

200 The soul rescuer

202 John Edward

208 Interpreting the spirits

210 The Ouija board

215 Chapter 5 – The uninvited: possession

217 The Vennum case

222 Soul music

227 The artist within

229 The three Claras

230 The question of reincarnation

235 Chapter 6 – Haunted houses

237 The Bloody Tower

244 The ghosts of Glamis

249 Pursued by dreams

251 Thirteen guests

255 Borley Rectory

258 The ghost-hunter's book

263 Weird night in a haunted house

267 The White House

270 Alcatraz

274 The Edgar Allen Poe house

276 Toys "R" Us

279 Chapter 7 – Spooky sites

281 Haunted hotel

285 The town too tough to die

289 Tombstone's spooky sites

291 A glimpse into the past

296 Sense of foreboding

300 Published, and damned

302 The ghosts of Glastonbury

307 Ghosts of the London Underground

312 Ghost flight

315 Haunted Hollywood

325 Their final bow

327 Spooked celebrities

330 Life imitating art

333 Celebrity seance

337 **Chapter 8 – Ghost hunters**

339 Harry Price – ghost hunter

346 Most haunted

354 Is your house haunted?

358 How to see a ghost

363 Speaking with spirits

366 The ghost hunter's tool kit

369 How to conduct a ghost hunt

376 Afterword

382 *Bibliography*

'The spirit world shuts
not its gates;
Your heart is closed,
your senses sleep'

Goethe

Introduction

'The spirit world shuts not its gates;
Your heart is closed, your senses sleep'

Goethe

This book is different from the usual collection of 'true' ghost stories. Although it offers a comprehensive history of spectral sightings from ancient times to the present day and covers apparitions in every conceivable setting, it does not argue the case for or against the existence of ghosts, but accepts apparitions as a natural phenomenon. Ghosts are a fact, but not all ghosts are discarnate spirits of the departed. The distinction is important and, as will be clear from the examples given in the following pages, goes to the core of explaining the nature of the phenomenon.

The reason for my unqualified conviction is not blind faith or wishful thinking, but personal experience. Since childhood I have had involuntary out-of-body experiences that are distinctly different from the most lucid of dreams and these have convinced me that our physical world is not the only reality. It was self-evident to me that we are, in essence, spiritual beings inhabiting a physical body and that we can be temporarily released from this shell when we attain a state of deep relaxation, during sleep, when under anaesthetic or at moments of extreme physical or emotional crisis.

I have had the privilege of working with many gifted 'sensitives' in my psychic development workshops. I have witnessed several remarkable demonstrations of medium-ship at first hand by well known and highly respected personalities such as Derek Acorah, Colin Fry, 'psychic detective' Chris Robinson and psychic surgeon Stephen Turoff. I have also interviewed many gifted individuals such as the healer Betty Shine and American 'psychic spy' Major David Morehouse, all of whom added to my understanding.

As I have explored the world of the supernatural I have become increasingly fascinated by what these phenomena reveal about our true nature and the greater reality of which we are a part, rather than by the phenomena themselves. What I hope distinguishes this book from others on the subject is an understanding that ghosts are not the chain-rattling spooks of lurid supernatural fiction, but something far more interesting. It will become evident from the many intriguing cases described in these pages that ghosts are not a single, specific phenomenon but cover a wide range of paranormal activity, each revealing another aspect of our latent psychic faculties and cultural conditioning.

We are naturally inclined to disbelieve anything outside our personal experience unless a case can be made for its existence on rational grounds. The root of Western scepticism towards all aspects of the supernatural is based on a fallacy expressed in the empiricist philosophy of David Hume (1711–76) who argued that only that which can be perceived through the senses should be accepted as real. He denied the possibility of miracles, for example, by loading the question even more cynically than might a modern politician. He asked whether it was more likely that witnesses would lie, or that the laws of nature would be violated? Hume failed to understand that paranormal phenomena do not violate or contradict nature; the supernatural is an extension of the natural world and conforms to universal laws.

Those who deny the evidence of such phenomena on principle would do well to consider the view of Carl Jung, the founding father of modern analytical psychology who expressed his belief in spirits in a letter to a friend:

'I once discussed the proof of identity for a long time with a friend of William James, Professor Hyslop in New York. He admitted that all things considered, all these metaphysic phenomena could be explained better by the hypothesis of spirits than by the qualities and peculiarities of the unconscious. And here, on the basis of my own experience, I am bound to concede he is right. In each individual case I must of necessity be sceptical, but in the long run I have to admit that the spirit hypothesis yields better results in practice than any other.'

In this book, I hope you will find answers to the most persistent questions regarding the nature of spirits rather than the vague and inconclusive statements which have tainted many previous investigations. I am not concerned here with the age-old argument for or against the existence of life after death as surely only the most stubborn sceptic would argue against the wealth of compelling experiential evidence on offer here and elsewhere. The more pressing question is whether we can shrug off the negative image we have of ghosts as malevolent entities created by centuries of superstition and lurid horror fiction and instead accept them simply as discarnate personalities on the other side of life. If this volume can contribute to a more commonsense approach to the supernatural and encourage even one person to lose their fear of the unknown then it will have served its purpose.

'Sit down before fact as a little child, be prepared to give up every preconceived notion, follow humbly wherever and to whatever abysses nature leads or you shall learn nothing.'

Thomas Henry Huxley on the duty of a scientist, 1860

CHAPTER 1

Belief in the soul

The belief in an immortal human soul
and its survival after death dates back
to prehistoric times and is common to
almost every culture around the world.

EVIDENCE for a belief in immortality can be found in ancient burial customs which reveal that our ancestors had an expectation of an afterlife and a respect for the memory of the dead. This reverence for the departed, which dates back to the Stone Age and possibly beyond, is the clearest evidence that primitive man possessed self-awareness long before he had formed the means of expressing it in words. Prehistoric cave paintings from Africa to Australia support the belief that early man had a strong intuitive link with the spirit world and attempted to communicate both with his ancestors and with animals through tribal elders, shamans, medicine men and, later, the high priests of the first civilizations. Despite, by present standards, the inherent cruelty and comparative lack of sophistication of these early societies, it is evident that they all shared a belief in spirits long before the concept of good and evil found expression in orthodox religion.

CULTS OF THE DEAD

The ancient Egyptians were so preoccupied with the prospect of an afterlife that their entire civilization was founded on the cult of the dead. Their custom of placing mummified corpses into sarcophagi of increasing refinement resulted from their belief that there are three non-physical components within the human body, (the *ka*, *ba* and *akh*) which equate with the etheric, astral or dream body of the Western esoteric tradition, the mind and the immortal soul. The etheric body is the non-physical counterpart that is effectively a blueprint for the form which our body takes on entering this material dimension.

Many believe that the pyramids may have been built not only as tombs for their pharaohs, who were venerated as living descendants of the Gods, but also as the means of initiation into the mysteries of life and death. According to this interpretation, their alignment with specific constellations was chosen to provide a path through the sky for the ascending spirit of the pharaoh to journey back to the heavens, specifically the Sirius constellation in the Milky Way whose river-like pattern of stars appeared to be a celestial reflection of the Nile. It is also feasible that the empty stone sarcophagus in the King's Chamber of the Great Pyramid at Giza was used to stimulate the conscious separation of the soul in order for the High Priests to be able to commune with the Gods. The structural shape of the pyramids was believed to have both a mystical significance and a practical purpose, focusing the Earth's magnetic energies to a specific point and to such effect that the initiate would be unable to resist the force drawing their etheric body out of its physical home. Earth energies are stronger near water which suggests one explanation of why the pyramids were built near the Nile. The theory was tested in the 1930s by English occultist Dr Paul

Brunton who spent the night in the King's Chamber and there experienced an involuntary astral journey.

> '... all my muscles became taut, after which a paralysing lethargy began to creep over my limbs. My entire body became heavy and numb... The feeling developed into a kind of iciness... All sensation in the lower limbs was numb. I appeared next to pass into a semi-somnolent condition...
>
> I felt myself sinking inwards in consciousness to some central point within my brain, while my breathing became weaker and weaker... There was a final mad whirl within my brain. I had the sensation of being caught up in a tropical whirlwind and seemed to pass upwards through a narrow hole; then there was the momentary dread of being launched into infinite space... I had gone ghost-like out of my earthly body.'

The Egyptian belief in the three spirit elements is significant because it has its equivalent in many cultures around the world which are different in virtually every other respect. It cannot be coincidence that the Greeks wrote of the significance of the *psyche*, the *pneuma* and the *nous*; the Muslims spoke of the *sirr*, *ruh* and *nafs*; the Hindus acknowledged the *atman*, *jiva* and *pranamayakosha*; while the Jewish mystics contemplated the nature of the *neshamah*, the *ruah* and the *nefash* which the Christians assimilated and externalized in the concept of the Holy Trinity.

Belief in a spirit double which can free itself from the body during sleep and exist separate from the body also gave rise to the Roman *larva*, the Tibetan *delok*, the German *doppelgänger*, the English *fetch*, the Norwegian *vardoger* and the Scottish *taslach*.

Today belief in a spirit double is shared by cultures as diverse as the Azande in Africa, the Inuit of Alaska and the Bacairis in South America as well as the major religions and philosophies of the East. Clearly there must be a basis in fact for this shared belief. It seems unlikely that mere wishful thinking or the desire to deny our own mortality could account for the consistency of such beliefs.

SACRED SPIRITS

In many parts of the world, ghosts are not considered to be a creation of local folklore, but a fact of life. In China the dead are understood to co-exist with the living, a belief which gave rise to the practice of ancestor worship, while in South America the deceased are honoured with annual festivals known as the Day of the Dead which suggests that the material world and the spirit world might not be as distinct as we might like to believe. In the Eastern and Asiatic religions it is believed that death is not the end, but simply a transition from one state of being to another. The Hindu *Upanishads*, for example, liken each human soul to a lump of salt taken from the ocean which must ultimately return to the source.

'*All the diverse elements, in the end, go back to the source*

*and are absorbed in it, as all waters are finally absorbed
in the ocean . . . A lump of salt may be produced by
separating it from the water of the ocean. But when it
is dropped into the ocean, it becomes one with the ocean
and cannot be separated again.'*

In Buddhism, the personality is believed to dissolve at
the moment of death leaving only pure consciousness
(*rupa*) to seek a new body unless the individual was an
enlightened soul (*bodhisattva*) in which case it can ascend
to the higher states of being and there choose when to
intervene in the lives of the living as a guiding spirit.
However, those individuals who are as yet unable to free
themselves from earthly attachments may descend into
the realm of the hungry ghosts, the Buddhist equivalent
of the Christian Hell.

It is implied that the majority of discarnate souls linger
in a limbo between lives, known as the *bardo*, before
reincarnating. The *Tibetan Book of the Dead* was intended
to act as a guidebook for the soul which found itself in

this transitional state. It was to be read over the dying and the dead who, it was thought, might be disorientated by finding themselves in this unearthly environment.

> *'The hour has come to part with this body, composed of flesh and blood; May I know the body to be impermanent and illusory.'*

Though it was written more than 1,000 years ago, its description of the three phases of death are uncannily similar to modern accounts of the near-death experience. The first stage, called *chikai bardo,* occurs when consciousness is suspended at the point of separation from the physical body. At this moment the individual is unaware that they are dead. Only when they look down on their own lifeless body do they realize that this ethereal essence is their true self.

> *'. . . thine intellect hath been separated from thy body. Because of this inability to loiter, thou oft-times wilt feel*

perturbed and vexed and panic-stricken . . . '
The *Tibetan Book of The Dead*, Evans-Wentz translation

There then follows a detailed description of the etheric body and its capabilities.

'Having a body [seemingly] fleshly [resembling] the former and that to be produced, Endowed with all sense faculties and power of unimpeded motion.'

The following passages stress the importance of letting go of all emotional attachments to people and places so that the soul may ascend into the light. But some may be unwilling, or unable, to relinquish their possessions or may harbour regrets or resentment which will effectively bind them to the earthly plane. Others may be literally haunted by their own evil deeds and they will only exorcize these memories by reliving them in a succession of hells of their own making.

'O now, when the Bardo of Reality upon me is
  dawning!
Abandoning all awe, fear, and terror of all
  phenomena,
May I recognise whatever appears as being my own
  thought-forms,
May I know them to be apparitions in the intermediate
  state'

Having faced the consequences of his actions, the discarnate soul can then submit to the mercy of the Buddha within, his own divine essence who determines whether he can enter Nirvana or must reincarnate. Assuming that most souls will need to return to the world for further trials, the concluding prayers are intended to guide it to re-enter under the most favourable circumstances.

'O procrastinating one, who thinks not of the coming of
  death,

Devoting yourself to the useless doings of this life,
Improvident are you in dissipating your great
opportunity;
Mistaken, indeed, will your purpose be now if you
return empty-handed from this life'

SPIRITS IN THE SCRIPTURES

The oldest recorded account of an encounter with a spirit in Western mythology can be traced back to the appearance of the Witch of Endor in the Old Testament who was ordered by King Saul to summon the spirit of the prophet Samuel.

Saul, the King of Israel, had condemned all occult practices as blasphemous, but when he heard that the Philistines were marching on the city of Gilboa he appealed to God for help. Receiving no answer he disguised himself and called on the witch who used a talisman to invoke the dead from the netherworld. The spirit of Samuel materialized out of the earth in the form of 'an old man . . . wrapped in a cloak' and complained of having been disturbed. Saul begged forgiveness and assured the spirit that he would not have disturbed him had his kingdom not been in peril to which Samuel replied that what is fated to befall men cannot be undone. The spirit then departed leaving Saul to face his enemies.

The story is seen by some as a satire on the king who is forced to acknowledge forces greater than those at his command, and it also serves as a moral fable. Saul deceived the witch (by coming to her in disguise), but she proved to be the wiser. After the spirit departed she showed compassion for the humbled ruler, killing one of her animals to feed him. The story also underlines the Jewish belief that the soul of the deceased hovers near its body for 12 months after death before ascending to heaven.

Communication with spirits was forbidden by the Old Testament (Deuteronomy 18:9–14), but conscious awareness of the higher worlds for the purpose of self-realization or enlightenment had been practised since biblical times by initiates of Merkabah, a forerunner of the modern Jewish mystical teaching known as Kabbalah.

Spirits are not acknowledged explicitly in the New Testament although their existence is clearly implied, most notably in Luke 24:39, when Jesus tells his followers: 'Touch me and make sure that I am not a ghost, because ghosts don't have bodies, as you see that I do!'

Elsewhere, particularly in the 'lost' Gnostic gospels discovered at Nag Hammadi in 1947, there are several significant references to the living spirit within every human being and to the disciples' personal experience of the astral world and altered states of awareness. In the Gospel of Philip, Jesus makes a clear distinction between 'the real realm' (i.e., the material world) and 'the realm of truth'.

'People cannot see anything in the real realm unless they become it. In the realm of truth it is not as [with] human

beings in the world, who see the sun without being the
sun . . . Rather, if you have seen any things there, you
have become those things.'

In 1 Corinthians 15:50 and 2 Peter 1:18 it is stated that
flesh and blood cannot enter the celestial kingdom; in
John 3:13 it is noted that heaven is for spiritual beings
and that we are all spirit in essence and will return from
whence we came:

'And no man hath ascended up to heaven, but he that
came down from the heaven, even the Son of man which
is in heaven.'

According to the Gnostic gospels, Jesus appeared to his
followers as a spirit to prove that the soul survives death,
but due either to selective editing of the gospels or a
mistranslation of the rich metaphorical language of the
Gnostic gospels, this central teaching became literalized.
St Paul attempted to clarify the idea that Jesus had

risen physically from the tomb and in so doing made a distinction between our earthly form and our spirit:

'There are also celestial bodies, and bodies terrestrial: but the glory of the celestial is one, and the glory of the terrestrial is another . . . There is a natural body and there is a spiritual body.' (1 Corinthians 15:35–44).

Elsewhere, in 2 Corinthians, St Paul speaks of having attained separation of the spirit and the body at will and having ascended 'in the spirit' to the third heaven, which was a technique he may have mastered as an initiate of an aesthetic sect of Jewish mystics who practised merkabah – an advanced form of meditation which translates as 'rising in the chariot'.

ANCIENT APPARITIONS

In order to understand the nature of ghosts we need to accept the fact that we all possess what is often called a dream body – an etheric or spirit double composed of subatomic matter connected to our physical form by an etheric umbilical cord which is only severed upon death. Such a concept is central to the philosophies of the East, but can seem too fanciful to those Westerners who have not had an out-of-body experience (OBE), or at least have no memory of the experience, for it is likely that everyone has had an OBE during the deepest stages of sleep.

So what evidence is there for the existence of this 'true self' and how might it explain the various phenomena we categorize under the broad heading of 'ghosts'? While much of the evidence is anecdotal, there are numerous cases where an apparition was witnessed by more than one person or where an individual was later able to verify details they had observed during their astral journey. There is also solid scientific evidence for the existence of the etheric double gathered from experiments conducted in the mid-1970s by Dr Karl Osis of California, USA during which the invisible presence projected by a psychic in an adjoining room was recorded either by photosensitive instruments or sensors which could detect the tiniest movements of a feather in a sealed container.

This question of evidence occupied the ancients as intensely as it continues to occupy us today. The earliest recorded discussion on the subject can be found in the writings of the Chinese philosopher, Mo Tzu (470–391 BC).

> *'Since we must understand whether ghosts and spirits exist or not, how can we find out? Mo Tzu said: The way to find out whether anything exists or not is to depend on the testimony of the ears and eyes of the multitude. If some have heard it or some have seen it then we have to say it exists. If no one has heard it and no one has seen it then we have to say it does not exist. So, then, why not go to some village or some district and inquire? If from antiquity to the present, and since the beginning of man, there are men who have seen the bodies of ghosts and spirits and heard their voices, how can we say that*

they do not exist? If none have heard them and none have seen them, then how can we say they do? But those who deny the existence of the spirits say: "Many in the world have heard and seen something of ghosts and spirits. Since they vary in testimony, who are to be accepted as really having heard and seen them? Mo Tzu said: As we are to rely on what many have jointly seen and what many have jointly heard, the case of Tu Po is to be accepted." Tu Po was minister to the Emperor Hsuan [827–783 BC] who ignored warnings that if he executed Po on false charges he would be haunted by the minister's ghost. Three years later Hsuan was killed with an arrow fired by an apparition resembling Tu Po in front of an asembly of feudal lords.'

Chapter 31, Yi-pao Mei translation

RESTLESS SPIRITS

The legend of Tu Po is clearly a moral fable and was widely accepted as such. In other parts of the world such stories became the basis for local myths, especially if there was a lesson to be learned. In South America, for example, there is the legend of the Weeping Woman who is said to have committed suicide after a handsome seducer refused to marry her as he had promised to do. She is said to haunt the highways in search of her children whom she had killed in order to be free to marry him. Her tale is told to young girls entering womanhood as a warning against believing the lies of men. In Japan there is a long tradition of apocryphal ghost stories in which wronged women return from the dead to take their revenge on those who have dishonoured them. The tale of the Tofu Seller is characteristic of this type of fable. It tells of a blind tofu vendor who is tricked into removing a charm from the door of a house by a wizened old hag who claims to be the ghost of the householder's first wife. Once the charm is removed, the ghost glides inside and a horrible scream is heard from within as the old hag frightens her husband's second wife to death.

The most persistent ghost story in Japanese culture

is the legend of the *Kuchisake-onna*, the spiteful spirit of a vain young girl who was the wife or concubine of a jealous samurai in the Heian period. Fearing that she had betrayed him with another man he is said to have disfigured her and then taunted her by saying: 'Who will think you're beautiful now?' Her face covered with a mask, the *Kuchisake-onna* wanders through the fog seeking solitary children, young men and women, whom she asks: '*Watashi kirei?*' (Am I beautiful?). If they answer 'yes' she tears off the mask and asks again. If they keep their nerve and again answer 'yes' she allows them to go on their way, but if they run screaming she pursues them, brandishing a long-bladed knife or a scythe. If she catches a man she butchers him and if she catches a girl she mutilates her, turning her into another *Kuchisake-onna*. The story is so deeply rooted in the Japanese psyche that as recently as 1979 there was public panic when it was rumoured that the *Kuchisake-onna* had been seen attacking children. In 2004, cities in South Korea were rife with similar rumours.

The earliest credible account of a spectral encounter was recorded by the Greek philosopher Athenodorus who lived during the 1st century BC. Against the advice of his friends, Athenodorus agreed to rent a room in a lodging house that was reputed to be haunted because it was cheap and he wished to prove that his actions were determined by his intellect and not his emotions. At nightfall his nerves were tested by the appearance of a gaunt-faced spirit of an old man draped in the soiled vestments of the grave. The spectre was weighed down by chains and appeared to be in anguish but was unable to communicate what it was that bound him to that place.

The philosopher kept his nerve and indicated that he was willing to follow the ghost wherever he wished to lead him. It led Athenodorus along a narrow passage and out into the garden whereupon it faded into the bushes. Athenodorus noted where the spirit had disappeared and the next morning he informed the magistrates who ordered workmen to excavate the garden. There they unearthed a skeleton weighed down by rusted chains which they assumed was that of a murder victim. They then had the skeleton reburied according to Greek funeral rites. Such stories have their counterpart in virtually every culture from ancient times to the present day.

The English ghost story tradition can be traced back to an episode involving Lord Lyttleton who, in 1779, claimed that he was tormented by the spirit of his jilted mistress, Mrs Amphlett, whose three daughters he had also seduced. She had committed suicide in despair and had returned to foretell the day and hour of his death. His friends, fearing for his sanity, thought they would try to outwit the spook by turning all the clocks forward. When the appointed hour passed without incident his lordship retired to bed much relieved and cursing himself for being a superstitious fool. But the dead are not so easily cheated and at the appointed hour Lord Lyttleton expired in his sleep from a fit.

CHAPTER 2

The night side of nature

The modern obsession with the supernatural
began in nineteenth-century New York
State when coded communications with a
restless soul gave birth to Spiritualism.

THE MODERN PREOCCUPATION with the paranormal could be said to have begun in 1848 with the publication of *The Night Side of Nature*. The Victorians were avid readers of ghost stories, but they bought this collection in unprecedented quantities because its author, Scottish novelist Catherine Crowe, appealed both to their romanticism and their reason. Her obvious delight in describing Gothic horrors was balanced with rigorous research. Each episode was backed up by witness statements, documents and dates to reinforce the author's belief that the supernatural was as worthy of serious investigation as the natural sciences. Her view was that the scientific establishment was arrogant and presumptuous in stating that all paranormal phenomena were the result of hysteria. It was her contention that the majority of scientists 'arrange the facts to their theory, not their theory to the facts'.

Crowe's timing was opportune. The belief in the infallibility of science was beginning to be questioned, yet the literate classes were also losing their faith in religion. Neither science nor religion appeared to have all the answers, but it seemed that a commonsense approach to the supernatural – and specifically to the question of life after death – might finally reconcile the two. By insisting that at least two independent witnesses corroborate each sighting, she laid down the ground rules for conducting paranormal research which was to change little over the next 100 years.

WILLINGTON MILL

Her most thorough and intriguing investigation concerned Willington Mill, near Newcastle-upon-Tyne, England, which was a haunted mill house owned by an industrialist, Joshua Proctor, who provided a sworn statement which Mrs Crowe included as a preface to her account. The property was only 40 years old when Proctor moved in during the spring of 1840, so it did not conform to the traditional idea of a house haunted by the spirits of previous owners. Moreover, Proctor was a devout Quaker, a God-fearing Christian not given to belief in spooks. And neither was Dr Edward Drury, a hardened sceptic and amateur ghostbuster who was the first on the scene when rumours of the haunting circulated around the region. It was Dr Drury who was to bring the facts to the attention of Mrs Crowe.

In July, Drury and his trusted friend Mr Hudson inquired if they could spend the night in the mill house in order to 'unravel the mystery', implying that they expected to expose a hoax. On meeting Mr Proctor they were immediately struck by his honesty and candour and so decided that they would not need the brace of loaded pistols with which they had intended to frighten the trickster. Proctor clearly believed that something was amiss and had even sent his family away so that the investigators could have a clear field.

At 11pm on the night of 3 July 1840, Dr Drury and his companion made themselves comfortable on a third floor landing outside the haunted room and settled down for an all-night vigil. At midnight they heard the sound of bare feet running across the floor, then knocking sounds as if someone was rapping with their knuckles on the bare boards. Other noises followed in quick succession – a hollow cough and a rustling – suggesting that a presence was making itself known. By 12.45 am, Dr Drury assumed that the show was over and was planning to retire to bed leaving Mr Hudson on the landing, but before he could do so Dr Drury saw a sight that was to haunt him for the rest of his life. A closet door swung open and 'the figure of a female, attired in greyish garments, with the head inclining downwards, and one hand pressed upon the chest as if in pain', strode slowly towards him. The spectre advanced towards Mr Hudson at which point the doctor found the courage to charge at it but he passed right through the apparition, knocking over his companion. Drury confesses that he recollected nothing for three hours afterwards and was assured by Hudson and Proctor that he was 'carried down stairs in an agony of fear and terror'. The good doctor was so traumatized by his experience that he required 10 days to calm his nerves before writing his account. He ended it by stating that he had gone there as a devout disbeliever but had emerged convinced of the reality of the supernatural.

Not content with relying on Dr Drury's account and Proctor's verification, Mrs Crowe dug deeper, unearthing accounts of earlier and subsequent sightings at Willington Mill given by four other people, plus a local newspaper proprietor and a historian who discovered that ghosts had been seen in a house that had occupied the same site 200 years earlier. Mrs Crowe wrote:

'The following more recent case of an apparition seen in the window of the same house from the outside, by four credible witnesses, who had the opportunity of scrutinising it for more than ten minutes, is given on most unquestionable authority. One of these witnesses is a young lady, a near connection of the family, who for obvious reasons, did not sleep in the house; another, a respectable man . . . his daughter . . . and his wife who first saw the object and called out the others to view it. The appearance presented was that of a bare-headed man in a flowing robe like a surplice, who glided backward and forward about three feet from the floor, or level with the bottom of the second story window seeming to enter the wall on each side and thus present a side view in passing. It then stood still in the window and a part of the body came through both the blind which was close down and the window, as its luminous body intercepted the framework of the window. It was semi-transparent and as bright as a star, diffusing a radiance all around. As it grew more dim it assumed a blue tinge and gradually faded away from the head downward. Had any magic lantern been used it could not possibly have escaped detection . . . '

Mrs Crowe travelled to Willington Mill to question the witnesses herself and found them to be entirely credible.

> *'They spoke of the facts above detailed with the simple earnestness of people who had no doubts whatever on the subject.'*

But although *The Night Side of Nature* can be credited with raising public awareness of paranormal phenomena and making a case for having the subject taken seriously, it was an event on the other side of the Atlantic which raised belief in the afterlife to such an extent that it became the foundation for a new religion – spiritualism.

THE FOX SISTERS

The event that led to the birth of the Spiritualist movement occurred in Hydesville, near Rochester, New York in the spring of 1848.

On 31 March, a Methodist farmer James Fox, his wife

Margaret and their two daughters, Margaretta aged 14 and Kate aged 12, retired early in the hope of catching up on their sleep. They had suffered several disturbed nights due to noises which they assumed were caused by the wind rattling the shutters of their wooden frame house. But the wind was not to blame. Before coming to bed Mrs Fox tried the sashes to see if they were loose and was answered by bangs for which there was no obvious explanation. Puzzled, she put the children to bed then prepared to retire herself. The family all slept in the same room and so Mrs Fox was a witness to what happened next. The rapping noises began again. Kate reminded them all that the next day was April Fool's Day and assumed that someone was playing a practical joke. She thought it might be fun to test them and challenged whoever was making the noises to copy her. She snapped her fingers and was immediately answered by the same number of raps. Then Margaret clapped and was answered in the same way. By now Mrs Fox was concerned as she knew that no one else but her husband could be in the house and he would not indulge in such frivolous games. She was also aware that a previous tenant had moved out after complaining of inexplicable noises. She later wrote:

> *'I then thought I could put a test that no one in the place could answer. I asked the noise to rap my different children's ages, successively. Instantly, each one of my children's ages was given correctly, pausing between them sufficiently long to individualise them until the seventh [child], at which a longer pause was made, and then three more emphatic little raps were given corresponding to the age of the little one that died . . . '*

Mrs Fox kept her composure, but she was increasingly anxious. She asked out loud if it was a human being making the noises. There was no reply. 'Is it a spirit?' she asked. 'If it is make two raps.' She was answered emphatically with two bangs that shook the house. In later weeks, disbelievers accused the children of making the noises by cracking their joints but it is reported that anyone who had heard the loud reports which shook the walls that first night would have dismissed such explanations out of hand.

Emboldened by her ability to converse with the other side, she then asked if it was an 'injured spirit' to which she received two loud raps in reply. Using an impromptu code, Mrs Fox elicited the following information from the intruder. It was the spirit of a 31-year-old man who had been murdered in the house and had left behind a widow and five children. Mrs Fox obtained permission from the spirit to invite the neighbours in to witness their exchange, but many were too frightened to enter the bedroom. They waited outside while a hard-headed pragmatist by the name of William Duesler sat on the end of the bed and quizzed the spirit with more personal questions. Duesler's cynicism melted the moment the bed vibrated in response to the strength of the rapping sounds.

Duesler managed to draw out more information

including the fact that the murdered man was a peddler by the name of Charles Rosma and that he had been killed five years earlier by a previous tenant of the house, a Mr Bell, for the $500 that he had saved and carried with him. Subsequent inquiries confirmed that a maid had been sent away on the evening a peddler had been invited to spend the night, and that when she returned the next morning the peddler had gone.

By Sunday, 2 April, rumours of what was taking place in the Fox family home were the topic of conversation around every breakfast and dinner table in the town. Hundreds of people converged on the house hoping to hear the raps and learn the latest news from the spirit world. Interest intensified when it was learnt that the murdered man had informed the family that his body had been buried in their cellar. Without delay James Fox and a number of men picked up picks and shovels and started digging up the dirt floor. The excavation had to be interrupted when they struck an underground stream, but a couple of months later the water had drained away and digging was resumed. Five feet down they struck a plank. Underneath they discovered human bone fragments and tufts of hair in a bed of quicklime.

Meanwhile, the previous owner, Mr Bell, had been traced to nearby Lyon, New York, but in anticipation of being accused of murder he had petitioned his neighbours to provide written testimony as to his good character. There was little that the law could do at this stage other than wait for more damning evidence to be unearthed – or for Mr Bell to be forced into making a confession by his conscience or by the persistent phantom. Curiously, the murdered man had predicted that his killer would never be brought to trial and it proved to be so.

But then, in November 1904, the cellar wall collapsed revealing the original wall behind it and between the two, a skeleton. Someone had evidently exhumed the body from its initial grave beneath the cellar floor and re-interred it behind a hastily built partition. The scene was reminiscent of a scene from Edgar Allan Poe. But who was the victim? Those who looked upon it were in no doubt, for next to the grisly find lay a peddler's tin box.

THE BIRTH OF SPIRITUALISM

The Fox family were the first people to become national celebrities in the field of spiritualism, simply by being in the right place at the right time. Not surprisingly, there were those who resented the attention they had attracted, specifically the Church authorities who were suspicious of anyone claiming direct communication with the dead. Under pressure from the Church and puritan elements within the Rochester community, three separate committees were set up in the following months to investigate the phenomena. They subjected the children to strip searches and tests in which they tied their ankles together and made them stand on pillows to isolate them from the floor, but still the rappings continued. All three committees concluded that the children attracted the anomalous activity even if they were not the cause of it. When the children were absent from the house, nothing happened. To save them from becoming a freak show attraction they were separated by their parents and sent away to stay with relatives. Kate went to live with her older sister Leah in Rochester and Margaretta lived with her brother in Auburn. Yet still the noises continued.

However, before anyone could claim that this proved that the children had somehow manufactured the sounds, the spirits raised the stakes. Leah's sceptical lodger, Calvin Brown, was pelted with objects by an invisible assailant while invisible hands prodded and pulled at guests in brother David's boarding house. More incredibly, a 16-year-old girl, Harriet Bebee, who visited the boarding house was disturbed to discover that the spirits followed her home to plague her and her family in a similar fashion. The Fox family were finally forced to abandon their besieged home and move to Rochester, but to their dismay the spirits pursued them to their new house where the rappings persisted. Some were so loud that they could be heard at the other end of town.

Such an epidemic of poltergeist ('noisy ghosts') activity suggests that at least some of the phenomena might have been produced by the children themselves – teenage girls have subsequently been found to be the origin of much psychokinetic activity (physical phenomena caused by involuntary discharges of psychic energy) due to physiological changes at puberty – rather than by the sudden incursion of angry spirits into one region of the country. However, it seems some of the mischievous antics can only be explained in terms of spirits. One such identified himself through decoded communications with Kate as a dead relative by the name of Jacob Smith. The deceased were evidently keen to communicate, but were limited to creating loud reports and throwing objects across a room. Attempts were made to create a more sophisticated alphabetical code using different knocks to identify specific letters but any form of communication which relied on a crude form of Morse code was laborious and unreliable. A new and more direct way had to be found. The answer lay in allowing the spirits to take over the body of a willing individual so that the spirit could speak through their voice boxes or guide their hand to write a message from the world beyond. This development was foreseen by an anonymous spirit in a message dictated to Isaac Post, a visitor to the Fox home in 1849.

'Dear friends, you must proclaim this truth to the world. This is the dawning of a new era; you must not try to conceal it any longer. God will protect you and good spirits will watch over you.'

The age of the medium was at hand.

A SURPLUS OF SPIRITS

Mediums were nothing new. Since prehistoric times shamans, witch doctors, holy men and priests had claimed to be able to commune with their ancestors and the gods. In some cases it is clear from the nature of their messages that they were expressing ideas from their own subconscious and that the gods from whom they channelled their laws and edicts could be seen to have been universal archetypes personifying aspects of their own psyche. Many however, appeared to be genuine channels for discarnate entities whose predictions and insights were later verified by subsequent events. But psychic sensitivity and its various manifestations – clairvoyance ('clear seeing'), clairaudience ('clear hearing') and clairsentience ('sensing an unseen presence') – are not the exclusive preserve of 'gifted' mystics. Everyone, to a greater or lesser degree, has the ability to attune to the presence of spirits.

In the wake of the Fox sisters' experience, hundreds of ordinary people across the United States and Europe began holding séances and many were shocked to discover that they too could produce loud reports and automatic writing, and move objects. More than 100 'mediums' appeared in Rochester alone in a single year. Newspaper reporters across the country were run off their feet chasing stories of spectral manifestations and levitating tables. One journalist scooped his rivals when he learnt that the Fox sisters were not the first to have experienced such phenomena.

Two brothers and a sister named Davenport who lived in Buffalo, New York, had been disturbed by loud reports and vibrations in 1846, but they did not understand their significance until they attended a séance held by the Fox family four years later. During one of their own séances, Ira Davenport was told by a spirit to fire a pistol. In the flare of the discharge, witnesses swore they saw the ghostly figure of a man with his finger wrapped around the trigger. After the shot, the pistol was snatched out of Ira's hand and it fell to the floor. The spectre, who identified himself as 'John King', subsequently entered the bodies of each of the brothers and spoke through them for all in the room to hear.

Soon spirits across the country were performing all

manner of 'tricks' for the amusement of spell-bound on-lookers: playing musical instruments, moving furniture, producing ectoplasm (a gelatinous substance drawn from the living essence of matter), manifesting objects in midair (apports) and even superimposing their faces on that of the medium – a phenomenon known as transfiguration. It was as if the disembodied had suddenly discovered a way to tear the veil between their world and this and were as excited and uninhibited as children who had just learned to ride a bike.

Spiritualism swiftly became a recognized religion. In spiritualist meetings a medium would deliver a sermon dictated from the spirit world and then pass on messages from the departed to the eager congregation. However, the more serious-minded members voiced concerns that nothing of a profound nature was ever communicated. The mysteries of life and death and the nature of the world beyond were rarely alluded to in anything other than the vaguest of terms. The spirits seemed preoccupied with mundane matters and 'unfinished business' on earth. It was if they were trapped in a limbo between the worlds, unable to move on so long as their loved ones refused to let them go. For the bereaved it was undoubtedly comforting to be given indisputable evidence of survival in the form of personal information that no one else but the deceased could have known, but for those seeking answers to life's mysteries it was ultimately unsatisfying. Perhaps spiritualism wasn't the breakthrough it had promised to be.

Needless to say, the Church was outraged and condemned all communication with the beyond as dabbling with the devil. As their pews emptied they took courage from the numerous accounts of fake mediums who had been exposed by the press and they vented their righteous indignation on those fraudsters who had preyed on the bereaved and the gullible. But despite the damage done to its reputation, the new movement continued to spread at a phenomenal rate. Even Queen Victoria and Prince Albert declared themselves convinced after enjoying a table-turning (the manipulation of a table during a séance, attributed to spirits) session at one of their country retreats. While some treated a séance as nothing more than a fashionable new party game to amuse their dinner guests, and the scientific establishment dismissed the whole business on principle, there was also a sense that something significant had come to light. Perhaps science and religion no longer had all the answers.

THE HAUNTING OF CHARLES DICKENS

The Victorians were very fond of ghost stories and the most popular authors of the period relished competing with one another to see who could make their readers' flesh creep the most. One of the era's best-loved storytellers was Charles Dickens, though surprisingly the author of *A Christmas Carol, Oliver Twist* and many supernatural short stories on ghosts was not a believer in the paranormal. Dickens was a hardened sceptic until he had a disquieting paranormal experience of his own.

In 1861, Dickens contributed a ghost story to the popular magazine *All The Year Round* which centred on an encounter between a portrait painter and a young lady in a railway carriage. During the journey, the story goes, the pale looking lady inquired as to whether the artist could paint a portrait from memory to which he replied that he probably could. When asked the reason for her question she responded, 'Look at me again. You may have to take a likeness of me.' Shortly afterwards they parted and the painter travelled on to his destination. Two years later, an elderly gentleman by the name of Wylde called on the artist and asked if he would accept a commission to paint a portrait of his daughter from a description as she was not available to sit for the portrait in person for she had died some time earlier. Puzzled but intrigued the artist agreed and began to sketch a young lady in accordance with Mr Wylde's description. After several failed attempts to capture her likeness he was on the verge of giving up when in desperation he recalled the young woman whom he had met on the train and used her as his inspiration. 'Instantly, a bright look of recognition and pleasure lighted up the father's face,' Dickens wrote, 'and he exclaimed, "That is she!"' In the course of conversation, the artist asked when the young lady had died and was told it was two years previously on September 13 – the very date the painter had met the pale young woman on the train.

Such twists were almost clichés even in Victorian fiction, but what makes this particular story significant is that it was to have a resonance in real life. Shortly after publication, Dickens received an irate letter from a painter who claimed that the story was not fiction, but fact. It had been his own personal experience which he had written down with the intention of submitting it for publication, but had delayed and he was now convinced that Dickens had heard his story somehow and copied it – even down to the date chosen for the girl's death. The painter had told the story to his friends but had never mentioned the date until the time he wrote it all down. This is what particularly unnerved Dickens. He later wrote, 'Now my [original] story had *no date*; but seeing when I looked over the proofs the great importance of having a date, I wrote in, unconsciously, the exact date on the margin of the proof!'

GHOST LIGHTS

Not all spirits appear in human form. Often entities will register on video film and photographs as moving lights. The following true story recorded by the Reverend Charles Jupp, warden of a Scottish orphanage, in 1878 is of great interest because it was seen by two witnesses both of whom found its presence reassuring.

'As near as I can tell I fell asleep about 11 o'clock, and slept soundly for some time. I suddenly awoke without any apparent reason, and felt an impulse to turn round, my face being turned towards the wall, from the children. Before turning, I looked up and saw a soft light in the room. The gas was burning low in the hall, and

the dormitory door being open, I thought it was probable that the light came from the source. It was soon evident, however, that such was not the case. I turned round, and then a wonderful vision met my gaze. Over the second bed from mine, and on the same side of the room, there was floating a small cloud of light, forming a halo the brightness of the moon on an ordinary moonlit night.

I sat upright in bed looking at this strange appearance, took up my watch and found the hands pointing at five minutes to one. Everything was quiet, and all the children sleeping soundly. In the bed, over which the light seemed to float, slept the youngest of the . . . children mentioned above.

I asked myself, "Am I dreaming?" No! I was wide awake. I was seized with a strong impulse to rise and touch the substance, or whatever it might be (for it was about five feet high), and was getting up when something seemed to hold me back. I am certain I heard nothing, yet I felt and perfectly understood the words – "No, lie down, it won't hurt you." I at once did what I felt I was told to do. I fell asleep shortly afterwards and rose at half-past five, that being my usual time.

At 6 . . . I began dressing the children beginning at the bed farthest from the one in which I slept. Presently I came to the bed over which I had seen the light hovering. I took the little boy out, placed him on my knee, and put on some of his clothes. The child had been talking with the others; suddenly he was silent. And then, looking me hard in the face with an extraordinary expression, he said, "Oh Mr Jupp, my mother came to me last night. Did you see her?" For a moment I could not answer the child. I then thought it better to pass it off, and said, "Come, we must make haste, or we shall be late for breakfast."'

The incident prayed on Jupp's mind and perhaps it was guilt at not having reassured the child that later compelled him to write an account of that night for the orphanage magazine. When the child read it his expression changed and looking up at the Reverend he said, 'Mr Jupp, that is me.' Jupp answered, 'Yes, that is what we saw.' Satisfied that he had not dreamt it the child fell into deep thought, 'evidently with pleasant remembrances, for he smiled so sweetly to himself,' recalled Jupp, 'and seemed to forget I was present.'

THE GHOST CLUB

It has been said that if two Englishmen found themselves marooned on a desert island, the first thing that they would do would be to form a club. In 1873, two eminent English academics did just that after finding themselves isolated on an island of doubt surrounded by a sea of certainty.

Professor Henry Sedgwick of Trinity College, Cambridge, had earlier resigned his fellowship because he no longer felt he could subscribe to the Thirty-Nine Articles of Faith central to the Church of England. He was later reinstated when the religious qualifications for the fellowship were rescinded, but his disillusionment was deep rooted and he no longer felt able to accept what the rest of Christian society accepted in blind faith. Inevitably, his adoring students began to side with their mentor, among them Frederick Myers, the son of a clergyman.

One crisp winter's evening in 1869, Myers called on the professor and persuaded him to take a walk to discuss their reservations regarding religion. As they looked up at the stars Myers voiced his frustration with philosophy and idly asked if his companion had given any thought to the rise of spiritualism and if it might signify a breakthrough in man's understanding of the universe. Sedgwick was doubtful but a seed had been planted that was later to grow into the Society for Psychical Research (SPR), an informal collective of intellectuals and the restlessly inquisitive formed by Myers and his former mentor. Its stated aim was to investigate all forms of paranormal phenomena in a strictly scientific manner and settle the matter once and for all. Its strength was that its members included sceptics as well as believers, among them two future prime ministers – Arthur Balfour and William Gladstone – the poet Alfred Lord Tennyson, novelist Mark Twain, intellectual and critic John Ruskin and academic Charles Dodgson (better known as Lewis Carroll). The SPR investigated more than 700 paranormal incidents from telepathy to out-of-body experiences which they compiled in an exhaustive 2,000 page study published in several volumes as *Phantasms of the Living* in 1886.

During the four years of intense research prior to publication, Myers, who is credited with coining the term telepathy, attended several séances without success until, one evening, as he sat in a circle with the medium Charles Williams, a disembodied hand materialized in midair. Such phenomena had been faked by other psychics who had resorted to paying an assistant to appear in a darkened room dressed in black with only their hand exposed. Fearing another fake, Myers had grasped the phantom hand and felt it grow steadily smaller until it disappeared altogether like a deflating balloon, only there was nothing in his fist when he unclenched it. Myers concluded, 'Whatever else a "ghost" may be, it is probably the most complex phenomenon in nature . . . Instead of describing a "ghost" as a dead person permitted to communicating with the living let us define it as a manifestation of persistent personal energy.' It was Myers' belief that phantoms were not physical in the sense that they were solid, but occupied a physical space in a fourth dimension.

A GHOSTLY INTRUDER

The following is typical of the type of ghost stories the society investigated. It is significant because it was one of the rare occasions when a ghost was heard to speak, and also was so solid as to cast a shadow. Its appearance was witnessed by two people and supported by their signed statements along with those of another couple to whom they had told their story shortly after it had happened.

A married couple, who chose to be identified in the report as Mr and Mrs P (but whose real identity and address are on file in the SPR archives), were in bed when Mrs P was startled to see a stranger standing at the foot of the bed. He was dressed in a naval officer's uniform. She woke her husband who demanded to know what the man was doing in their bedroom at night. The officer simply spoke the husband's name as if reproving him for being so readily offended and then turned about and walked through the facing wall.

Mrs P had assumed that it prefigured some disaster for her brother who was in the navy, but her husband recognized the intruder as his father who had died several years earlier. Shortly afterwards, Mr P fell ill and remained in a serious condition for several weeks. When he recovered he confessed to his wife that he had accumulated a considerable debt and was so desperate that he had been considering going into business with a disreputable character whom he now realized might have ruined him for certain. He had taken his father's appearance and remonstration as a warning and was now determined to resolve his financial difficulties by himself.

CONCERN FROM BEYOND THE GRAVE

After the Great War, paranormal research was almost exclusively pursued by elderly academics and matronly mediums, but in February 1932 two investigators from the SPR arrived in the English village of Ramsbury, Wiltshire, to investigate a local haunting only to discover that the local vicar had beaten them to the story.

The grandchildren of chimney sweep Samuel Bull had complained that they could not sleep because they were aware of a presence outside their damp and dilapidated cottage. The case is noteworthy because the whole family witnessed the apparition on several occasions and instinctively reacted to it without prompting from the others.

Bull had died the previous summer but on several occasions his ghost appeared in full view of the children, their mother, Mary Edwards and Samuel's invalid wife, Jane, who lived with them. They saw him walking across the living room, up the stairs and through the closed door of the bedroom where he had died. At first they were all terrified, but they gradually became used to seeing the old man and were curiously reassured by his presence. He didn't look like a ghost and it was clear that he was aware of their presence. On two occasions he put his hand on Jane's head and spoke her name, but there was a sadness in his expression which the family assumed was his reaction to seeing them living in such squalid conditions. Shortly before the hauntings ceased Mrs Edwards received news that they were to be re-housed and thereafter the spectre of Samuel Bull appeared with a less troubled look on his face. When they moved he did not appear to them again.

SUICIDE SIGHTING

The SPR were scrupulous in their methods and, in an effort to satisfy their most hostile critics who were within their own ranks, subjected every case to the degree of scrutiny usually reserved for the natural sciences. Several of their members were distinguished physicists and guarded their reputations as staunchly as the clergy protected the sanctity of the Church. They were not interested simply in collecting ghost stories in the manner that amateur historians collected folklore. They were in search of incontrovertible evidence and that meant securing the written testimony of as many witnesses as possible. The following case is a prime example of the kind of incident they were keen to include.

One pleasant summer evening, a mother and her son were sitting in the back garden of their suburban house in Clapham, South London, when the young man exclaimed with surprise, 'Look mother, there's Ellen!' Ellen was the elder of his two sisters and had been sent to Brighton on the south coast by her parents to cool her heels after she had been forbidden to see an unsuitable suitor. The young lady was at the far end of the lawn walking toward the garden gate which led to the fields beyond. Fearing that her father might see her before she had a chance to explain her daughter's unexpected return, the mother asked her son to go after Ellen and bring her back to the house. 'I can't run after her,' he reminded her. He had sprained his ankle earlier that day. 'You'll have to send Mary.' So the mother called her younger daughter from the house and told her to run after Ellen and bring her back before her father saw her. They would send her back to Brighton in the morning without him knowing anything about it and so they would avoid an unpleasant scene.

Mary ran across the lawn and through the gate calling her sister's name, but Ellen did not respond. She continued to walk down a path across the fields leading away from the house, her black cloak billowing in the breeze. 'Ellen, where are you going?' asked Mary as she finally caught up with her sister. Then, as she grasped her sister's arm, she found her hand passing right through the apparently solid figure as through a mist. When she had collected herself, she walked back in a daze to where her mother and brother were waiting and told them what she had seen and that she feared the worse. The next day the family learnt that Ellen had thrown herself into the sea and drowned at the very hour that she had appeared to them in the garden.

LAST WILL AND TESTAMENT

One of the most famous and convincing accounts of survival after death preserved in the SPR archives described an occurrence on the other side of the Atlantic in 1885. An American farmer, Michael Conley of Chicasaw County, died of natural causes at an old people's home and was stripped of his filthy work clothes at the Dubuque County morgue. When his daughter was informed of his death she fainted, but when she recovered consciousness she claimed that her father had appeared to her and told her to recover a roll of dollar bills he had sewn into the lining of his grey shirt. Remarkably, she was able to describe the clothes he had been wearing at the time of his death, even down to the fact that he had wrapped the money in a square of red cloth torn from one of her old dresses. No one believed her, attributing her 'delusion' to grief, but to calm her down they decided to humour her by fetching the clothes from Dubuque and allowing her to examine them. In the lining of the grey shirt, wrapped in a patch of red cloth, they found the money just as the daughter had said they would.

A similar incident was recorded 40 years later by the American branch of the SPR. In Davie County, North Carolina, James Chaffin, a farmer's son, dreamt that his dead father appeared at his bedside and urged the boy to look for his missing will in the pocket of the overcoat that he was wearing in the dream. When James awoke he was puzzled as the farm had been left to the elder of his three brothers, Marshall Chaffin, according to the terms of the one and only will that the family had been aware of. Besides, the old man had been dead for four years. Why had he appeared now when the matter had long been settled? His curiosity aroused, James visited his mother and asked about the coat. She told him that it had been given to his brother John. John dutifully handed it over and was witness to what happened next. James tore open the lining of the inside pocket and inside found a message in his father's handwriting. It said, 'Read the 27th chapter of Genesis in my daddy's old Bible.'

Returning to his mother's house James found the family Bible and exactly at the place indicated they found the missing will. It had been written after the one that had left the farm to Marshall and expressed the father's wish that the land be divided equally between his widow and the four boys. Initially, Marshall was inclined to contest it, but backed down when 10 witnesses testified that it was in the old man's own handwriting.

When the case came to the attention of the SPR, they hired a lawyer to investigate it and he concluded that all the facts were correct. Old man Chaffin had chosen the 27th chapter of Genesis to make a point. It described how Jacob deceived his blind father Isaac into giving him what rightly belonged to his brother Esau. Unfortunately, the family were not habitual Bible readers and so the father was forced to make a belated appearance in order to ensure his last wish was respected.

A DISPIRITING RESPONSE

Phantasms of the Living presented a formidable accumulation of similar cases to convince many hardened sceptics. Although the general public was deterred from reading it by the mass of witness testimony and dry scholarly discussions regarding the validity of the evidence, several devout sceptics were converted. Professor James Hyslop, who was disliked by his fellow SPR members for his entrenched cynicism, felt compelled to urge other sceptics to admit defeat.

> *'I regard the existence of discarnate spirits as scientifically proved and I no longer refer to the sceptic as having any right to speak on the subject. Any man who does not accept the existence of discarnate spirits and the proof of it is either ignorant or a moral coward.'*

Nevertheless, the scientific establishment was un-impressed. It was not that they did not accept the evidence, but rather that they lost interest in phenomena since apparitions and apports did not add to their understanding of the inner workings of nature. As the novelist Nathaniel Hawthorne observed after having compiled convincing evidence purporting to prove the existence of the paranormal:

> 'These soberly attested incredibilities are so numerous that I forget nine tenths of them . . . they are absolutely proved to be sober facts by evidence that would satisfy us of any other alleged realities: and yet I cannot force my mind to interest itself in them.'

And this attitude has been the bane of believers ever since. Phenomena in themselves tell us nothing about the nature of the universe or human potential. No amount of table-turning, inexplicable rapping sounds or phantom materializations add to our understanding, only to the catalogue of anomalies. In the end a person either believes in ghosts or they do not. Those who were inclined to disbelieve may have been converted by the wealth of experiential evidence, but unless they had been disillusioned with their religion and felt fired up by spiritualism they might be inclined to say, 'All right, ghosts exist, but so what? What does it all mean?'

TIME DELAYED PROOF

The fact that *Phantasms of the Living* was not a bestseller did not dampen SPR members' enthusiasm, nor lessen their conviction that they were on the threshold of a new world and they were braced for a radical new understanding of the universe. The first study was only 'the foundation stone', as Myers liked to call it. A second study was hastily commissioned under the title *Census of Hallucinations* and attracted an astonishing 17,000 replies from individuals as far apart as Russia and Brazil. It appeared that the SPR had breached a dam. Paranormal experiences were more common than even the SPR had imagined, but many people had felt unable to admit to having had such experiences. Now the SPR and the spiritualists made it socially acceptable to talk about such things. Again, the most persuasive evidence was the cases confirmed by several witnesses. The following incident must rank as one of the most convincing cases ever recorded.

On the night of 3 January 1856, a New Jersey housewife, Mrs Anne Collye, awoke to see her son Joseph standing in the doorway of her bedroom in a dreadful state. He had severe head injuries which had been hastily wrapped in bandages and he was wearing a soiled white nightshirt. A moment later he vanished. Her family comforted Mrs Collye as best they could, reminding her that Joseph was 1,000 miles away in command of a Mississippi steamboat and that it must have been a nightmare brought on by worry. However, Mrs Collye protested that she had been wide awake. It wasn't until two weeks later that the family learned that Joseph had been killed in a collision with another boat. The mast on his vessel had fallen, splitting his skull on the very night she had seen her son standing in the doorway. When Joseph's brother viewed the body, he found it still wrapped in the soiled white nightshirt Joseph had been wearing when called from his cabin in the middle of the night to attend to the disaster. Fortunately for the SPR, Mrs Collye had described her experience to her husband and four daughters the next morning, a full two weeks before news reached them of the tragedy.

FRAUDS AND FAKES

Sadly, the society's efforts to bring such evidence to the attention of the scientific establishment were fatally undermined by several well-publicized scandals involving fake mediums. These occurred just prior to, and in the years immediately after, publication of *Census of Hallucinations* and consequently public ardour towards spiritualism was dampened and the sceptics had further cause to doubt. Several SPR members were duped by hoaxers who exploited their eagerness to believe, leaving the reputation of the society irreparably damaged by the turn of the century. The episode gave rise to the saying, 'for those who believe, no proof is necessary; for those who doubt, no proof is enough.'

Though their pride had been punctured SPR members continued to pursue their investigations independently, producing some of the most significant and influential studies of the period. Sir Oliver Lodge, twice president of the SPR, recorded his communications with his dead son Raymond in a bestselling book of the same name. Raymond had been killed at Ypres in August 1915 and Sir Oliver required incontestable evidence that his son's spirit survived his physical death. He received it in a remarkable way.

Sir Oliver's wife, Lady Lodge, was eventually persuaded to attend a séance presided over by a medium who did not know her by name and who was unaware of her situation. During the evening the medium, Mrs

Leonard, declared that she had a message from a young man named Raymond who had recently passed over and that he had met several of his father's friends including a man named Myers. Frederick Myers had died in 1901 and *Phantasms of the Living* had been published posthumously.

'Raymond' reappeared at a second séance held by a male medium, Vout Peters, during which he referred to a recent photograph in which Raymond was shown with a group of friends holding a walking stick. Raymond's parents did not possess such a photograph so Sir Oliver took the opportunity to raise the subject with Mrs Leonard on a subsequent visit. He was told that it had been taken outdoors and showed a comrade leaning on Raymond for support. A few days later a photograph arrived in the post from the mother of one of Raymond's fellow officers. She had known nothing of the séances, but had sent the photo to Lady Lodge because she had just learnt of Raymond's death. She realized that it must have been the last photo taken of her son. It showed

Raymond sitting in the front row with a walking stick by his side and another officer standing behind, leaning on his shoulders.

SPECTRAL SOLDIERS

During the First World War, both the Germans and the Allies reported several sightings of spectral soldiers who intervened to save the lives of their comrades. The most famous was the legendary 'Angels of Mons', which may have been the creation of the English novelist Arthur Maachen. However, the following story is generally considered to be authentic. It appeared in the August 1919 issue of the popular *Pearson's Magazine* and was credited to Captain W.E. Newcome.

'It was in September, 1916, that the 2nd Suffolks left Loos to go up into the northern sector of Albert. I accompanied them, and whilst in the front line trenches of that sector I, with others, witnessed one of the most remarkable occurrences of the war.

About the end of October, up to November 5th, we were actually holding that part of the line with very few troops. On November 1st the Germans made a very determined attack, doing their utmost to break through. I had occasion to go down to the reserve line, and during my absence the German attack began.

I hurried back to my company with all speed, and arrived in time to give a helping hand in throwing the enemy back to his own line. He never gained a footing in our trenches. The assault was sharp and short, and we had settled down to watch and wait again for his next attack.

We had not long to wait, for we soon saw Germans again coming over No Man's Land in massed waves; but before they reached our wire a white, spiritual figure of a soldier rose from a shell-hole, or out of the ground about one hundred yards on our left, just in front of our wire and between the first line of Germans and ourselves. The spectral figure then slowly walked along our front for a distance of about one thousand yards. Its outline suggested to my mind that of an old pre-war officer, for it appeared to be in a shell coat, with field-service cap on its head. It looked, first, across at the oncoming Germans, then turned its head away and commenced to walk slowly outside our wire along the sector that we were holding.

Our SOS signal had been answered by our artillery. Shells and bullets were whistling across No Man's Land . . . but none in anyway impeded the spectre's progress. It steadily marched from the left of us till it got to the extreme right of the sector, then it turned its face right full on to us. It seemed to look up and down our trench, and as each Véry light [flare] rose it stood out more prominently. After a brief survey of us it turned sharply to the right and made a bee-line for the German trenches. The Germans scattered back . . . and no more was seen of them that night.

The Angels of Mons seemed to be the first thought of the men; then some said it looked like Lord Kitchener, and others said its face, when turned full on to us, was not unlike Lord Roberts. I know that it gave me personally a great shock, and for some time it was the talk of the company. Its appearance can be vouched for by sergeants and men of my section.'

Later in the same article, another officer, William M. Speight, describes seeing the phantom figure in his dug-out that night. The next evening Speight invited another officer to serve as a witness in the hope that the vision might make another appearance. The dead officer duly appeared, pointed to a spot on the floor of the dug-out, then vanished. Intrigued and somewhat superstitious, Speight ordered a hole to be dug at the spot. To the amazement of Speight and the whole company, the sappers unearthed a narrow tunnel that had been excavated by the Germans, primed with mines timed to explode 13 hours later. The timers and explosives were excavated safely and destroyed.

From the numerous accounts of spectral soldiers on file it would seem that fighting men take such sightings in their stride. No doubt frayed nerves, fatigue and the proximity of death play their part in lowering the threshold of awareness which protects ordinary people from glimpsing the world beyond. In his memoirs of the First World War, the English poet Robert Graves recalled a sighting which produced only mild curiosity, rather than fear, at the time.

'I saw a ghost at Bethune. He was a man called Private Challoner who had been at Lancaster with me and again in F Company at Wrexham. When he went out with a draft to join the First Battalion, he shook my hand and said: "I'll meet you again in France, sir." He was killed at Festubert in May and in June he passed by our C Company billet where we were just having a special dinner to celebrate our safe return from Cuinchy . . . Challoner looked in at the window, saluted and passed on. There was no mistaking him or the cap badge he was wearing. There was no Royal Welch battalion billeted within miles of Bethune at the time. I jumped up and looked out of the window, but saw nothing except a fag

end smoking on the pavement. Ghosts were numerous
in France at the time.'

Years later Graves was asked what he thought ghosts might
be and he elaborated in the same dispassionate manner.

'I think that one should accept ghosts very much as
one accepts fire – a common but equally mysterious
phenomenon. What is fire? It is not really an element, not
a principle of motion, not a living creature – not even a
disease, though a house can catch it from its neighbours.
It is an event rather than a thing or a creature. Ghosts,
similarly, seem to be events rather than things or creatures.'

A 'STRANGE MEETING'

One of the finest poets of the First World War,
Wilfred Owen – who is perhaps best remembered for
his atmospheric verse 'Strange Meeting' in which a
German and a British soldier encounter each other in

the underworld – was killed just one week before the Armistice was declared. On the day the guns finally fell silent, his brother Harold, a naval officer, was overwhelmed by a feeling of apprehension and was later 'visited' in his cabin by Wilfred's spirit. Harold's reaction to the presence of his brother contrasts with the fears of fictional characters who are confronted by unquiet spirits and for that reason his experience is strangely comforting. Harold was unaware of his brother's death at the time of their strange meeting.

'I had gone down to my cabin thinking to write some letters. I drew aside the door curtain and stepped inside and to my amazement I saw Wilfred sitting in my chair. I felt shock run through me with appalling force and with it I could feel the blood draining away from my face. I did not rush towards him but walked jerkily into the cabin – all my limbs stiff and slow to respond. I did not sit down but looking at him I spoke quietly: "Wilfred how did you get here?" He did not rise and I

saw that he was involuntarily immobile, but his eyes which had never left mine were alive with the familiar look of trying to make me understand; when I spoke his whole face broke into his sweetest and endearing dark smile. I felt no fear – I had not when I first drew my door curtain and saw him there; only exquisite mental pleasure at thus beholding him. All I was conscious of was a sensation of enormous shock and profound astonishment that he should be here in my cabin. I spoke again, "Wilfred dear, how can you be here, it is just not possible . . . " But still he did not speak but only smiled his most gentle smile. This not speaking did not now as it had done at first seem strange or even unnatural; it was not only in some inexplicable way perfectly natural but radiated a quality which made his presence with me undeniably right and in no way out of the ordinary. I loved having him there: I could not and did not want to try to understand how he had got there. I was content to accept him, that he was here with me was sufficient. I could not question anything, the meeting in itself was complete and strangely perfect. He was in uniform and I remember thinking how out of place the khaki looked among the cabin furnishings. With this thought I must have turned my eyes away from him; when I looked back my cabin chair was empty . . .

I felt the blood run slowly back to my face and looseness into my limbs and with these an overpowering sense of emptiness and absolute loss . . . I wondered if I had been dreaming but looking down I saw that I was still standing. Suddenly I felt terribly tired and moving to my bunk I lay down; instantly I went into a deep and oblivious sleep. When I woke up I knew with absolute certainty that Wilfred was dead.'

THE CONVERSION OF CONAN DOYLE

Sir Arthur Conan Doyle, creator of the fictional detective Sherlock Holmes, became an enthusiastic advocate of spiritualism in the early days of the First World War. This was much to the dismay of his closest friends and most ardent admirers, among them King George V, Prime Minister Lloyd George and Winston Churchill. They were appalled that the man who had created the very embodiment of deductive reasoning should dabble with the specious world of spirits. They suspected it was due to his inability to cope with the death of his son Kingsley who had been killed in France, and his father, but Doyle's enthusiasm for the new fad had been awakened by a remarkable personal experience.

The author and his wife had been nursing a young lady, Lily Loder-Symonds, who was in poor health and spent much of her time practising automatic writing. Doyle was fascinated but had attributed the messages to the action of Lily's subconscious mind until one morning, in May 1915, she declared in some agitation that she had received a warning of impending disaster. 'It is terrible. Terrible. And will have a great influence on the war.' Later that day there came news that the transatlantic liner the Lusitania had been sunk by a German submarine with the loss of more than a 1,000 lives, 128 of them American. It was the turning point of the war. Americans were outraged and shortly after entered the war on the side of the Allies. Germany's fate was sealed.

Doyle began to take an active interest in 'spirit messages' after this and received what he considered to be incontrovertible proof of the soul's survival after death. It came in the form of a 'conversation' with his dead brother-in-law, Malcolm Leckie, who had been killed at Mons in April 1915. Doyle was stunned to witness Lily writing in Malcolm's unmistakable hand and struck up a dialogue during which he asked probing personal questions which only his brother-in-law could have known, relating to details of a private conversation which they had just before Malcolm returned to the front. Doyle had not even confided the gist of the conversation to his wife so Lily could not have learned about it from her hostess.

Doyle's interest in the paranormal intensified as he investigated the phenomenon and brought his conversion from agnostic to ardent believer to public attention. He became an active member of the Society for Psychical Research and attended many séances including one at which he heard the voice of his son and saw the revenants of his mother and nephew – an event witnessed by two independent observers. Galvanized by the experience, he embarked on a worldwide lecture tour to promote the cause to which he was now wholeheartedly committed. This was against the advice of his more sceptical friends and much to the derision of his less sympathetic readers. His own spirit photographs were pored over by fellow enthusiasts but were dismissed out of hand by critics who saw him as a credulous old fool taken in by fraudulent mediums.

Doyle shared the belief at the core of the spiritualist creed that the soul is an etheric blueprint of the body and that this explained why discarnate spirits assumed human form. In *The Vital Message*, he wrote:

'The physical basis of all psychic belief, is that the soul is a complete duplicate of the body, resembling it in the *smallest particular, although constructed of some far more tenuous material. In ordinary conditions these two bodies are intermingled so that the identity of the finer one is entirely obscured. At death, however, and under certain conditions in the course of life, the two can divide and be seen separately.'*

In 1926, he published *The History of Spiritualism,* the result of more than 10 years' research into the subject. The book made a convincing case for the existence of psychic phenomena while acknowledging that there were many fake mediums who had no scruples about fleecing the unwary. During the latter years of his life, Doyle befriended the illusionist Harry Houdini who was incensed by the crude parlour tricks employed by fake mediums and he was intent on exposing them. He and Doyle made an odd but amiable partnership – each with his own agenda – as they attended séances around the country. Ironically, they eventually fell out over Doyle's insistence on crediting Houdini's miraculous escapes to the illusionist's unconscious paranormal abilities, a theory he expounded in *The Edge of the Unknown*.

Ultimately, Doyle's credibility took a fatal blow after it was revealed that the Cottingley fairy photographs which he had publicly and enthusiastically declared to be genuine were in fact fakes, but his faith in the afterlife remained unshakable until his death in 1930.

THE PHANTOM FAYRE

In October 1916, Edith Olivier turned off the main road to Swindon in Wiltshire, in search of a public house in which she could spend the night. It was beginning to rain and she was in no hurry to reach her destination. As she peered through the darkness she saw ahead of her the imposing black monoliths which lined the road to the megalithic stone circle at Avebury. Despite the drizzle she was keen to see the site which at the time was rumoured to have been the scene of bacchanalian rituals in pagan times.

She stopped the car at the end of a long dirt road and climbed a small mound to get a better view. From here she could see a cluster of cottages in the middle of the circle and what appeared to be a village fayre in progress. From the sound of the laughter and the applause which greeted the fire eaters, acrobats and jugglers, the villagers were clearly enjoying themselves, undaunted by the weather. But then she noticed something peculiar. The fiery torches they carried were undimmed by the rain and not a single man, woman or child wore a raincoat nor carried an umbrella. It was as if they walked between the raindrops, indifferent to the drizzle which by now was becoming a steady downpour.

It was nine years before Edith visited the site again. On this occasion she was part of a guided tour and she took the first opportunity to ask the guide about the fayre. He confirmed that the villagers had held an annual fayre on the site, but the custom had stopped in 1850. It was then that Edith realized that the road approaching the mound she had stood upon was no longer there. No trace of it

been a long

but it had var

MASS MATER

While some appari

bound spirits, this ex

many sightings of ph

as the revellers seen by

conventional theory is that such souls are unaware

that they are dead and so continue to relive the drama

of their last hours as if trapped in a recurring dream.

While this may be true of certain stubbornly persistent

personalities, it seems unlikely that hundreds of

individual souls would reconvene on the anniversary

of their death to relive such an event. What would have

compelled the country folk of Avebury, for example, to

relive their night at the fayre if there was no tragedy that

had entrapped them? It seems more likely that sightings

involving a group are an ech

picked up by anyone

In short, the

again, the

and

Oliver at Avebury. The

or the

or groups such

... across time which can be ... possessing heightened perception. ... phantoms are not fighting their battles ... witness is simply tuning into it in their mind ... the stronger the emotional residue, the easier it is for one or more people to tune into it. If all phantom battles were genuine collective hauntings, most of Europe would echo to ghostly gunfire from dusk to dawn. Why, then, is one battlefield or village the setting for a spectral restaging and not another? Is it because the phantoms are mere ripples in the ether?

The best known example of a mass re-imagining is the phantom battle of Edgehill which was originally fought on 23 October 1642 between the Royalist Army of King Charles I and the Parliamentary Army commanded by Oliver Cromwell during the English Civil War. So violent was the clash that the ripples were seen and heard by the locals on consecutive weekends two months later.

Naturally, the king was perturbed when he heard rumours that his defeat was being replayed with the same ignominious result so he despatched three of his most loyal officers to see if there was any truth in the tales. They returned ashen faced to report that not only had they witnessed the re-enactment but that they had recognized several of their friends who had been killed on that day, as well as the king's nephew Prince Rupert who had survived.

It is tempting to dismiss such tales as the stuff of a more superstitious age, but such phenomena continue to be reported in more modern times. Two English women, holidaying in Dieppe, swore that they heard the sounds of a modern battle just before dawn on the morning of 4 August 1951. The sound of Stuka dive bombers, artillery shells and even the distinctive sound of landing craft hitting the beach was so loud they thought the French army were carrying out a training exercise or perhaps someone was making a war movie. But when they threw open the shutters of their hotel room they saw only empty streets. It was then that they remembered the significance of the date. On the same day nine years previously, a disastrous commando raid cost the lives of almost 1,000 Canadian soldiers.

CHAPTER 3

Living apparitions

If we want to understand what a ghost is,
we only need to look at living apparitions,
which include out-of-body experiences,
doppelgängers, crisis apparitions and
other ethereal phenomena.

After devoting much of his life to paranormal research, Sir Oliver Lodge came to the conclusion that ghosts were not conscious entities but emotional energy recorded in matter. He wrote:

'Take, for example, a haunted house wherein one room is the scene of a ghostly representation of some long past tragedy . . . the original tragedy has been literally photographed on its material surroundings, nay even on the ether itself, by reason of the intensity of emotion felt by those who enacted it; and thenceforth in certain persons an hallucinatory effect is experienced corresponding to such an impression. It is this theory that is made to account for the feeling one has on entering certain rooms, that there is an alien presence therein . . . '

THE STONE TAPE THEORY

This theory was to become known as the 'stone tape' theory, and may account for those sightings in which ghosts replay events from the most traumatic moments in their lives, exhibiting no conscious awareness of any witnesses who may be present. According to the hypothesis this type of ghost is merely an echo. But it does not explain the many incidents where apparitions of the living appear in one location while their body resides elsewhere. Neither does it explain how a living apparition can appear carrying an object, unless they have charged that object with their personal energy at the moment they are projecting their etheric body to the second location.

The SPR recorded a typical example of this in which a lady saw her uncle appear in her home carrying a roll of paper. She naturally assumed that he had decided to pay her a visit, but her uncle looked anxious as he strode across the room and out through an open door. By the time she had followed him outside he was nowhere to be seen. Later that day she received a letter from her father informing her that her uncle was gravely ill. He had died at the very same moment he had appeared in her home. As she stood by her uncle's bed, she felt an urge to look under his pillow and there she found a roll of paper on which, she assumed, he had intended to write a new will favouring her or her father.

It seems that the connection between the uncle's spirit and his body were weakening in the final moments of his life and so he was able to project his essence or his thought form to his niece's home. However, there are also well-documented cases of people who were in the best of health when they projected their image many miles away. The most famous example is that of the French school teacher Emilie Sagee.

IN TWO PLACES AT ONCE

Miss Sagee was a popular addition to the staff at the Neuwelcke finishing school for young ladies at Livonia (now Latvia) in 1845, but there was something unsettling about her which her pupils could not put into words. She was pretty, capable, conscientious but at the same time distracted, as if her mind was elsewhere. The trouble was that it was not only her mind that was elsewhere. So was her *doppelgänger*, her spirit double.

For weeks there had been rumours that Miss Sagee had been seen in two parts of the school at the same time. Naturally, her colleagues scoffed at the very idea and dismissed it as schoolgirl gossip, but they were soon forced to face the fact that there was more to Emilie than met the eye. One of her pupils, Antoine von Wrangel, was unusually anxious the day she prepared for a high society party. Even so, her girlish excitement cannot account for what she thought she saw when she looked over her shoulder to admire herself in the mirror. There, attending to the hem of her dress, was not one but two Mademoiselle Sagees. Not surprisingly the poor girl fainted on the spot. It became no longer a matter of rumour when a class of 13 girls saw Miss Sagee's *doppelgänger* standing next to its more solid counterpart at the blackboard one day, mimicking the movements of the 'real' Emilie.

However, no one could blame the teacher – she had done nothing improper. By now the whole school was on edge and rife with wild unfounded stories as the girls embellished their experiences for the entertainment of their friends. Eventually, these stories reached the ears of the headmistress, but there were no grounds for a reprimand, never mind a dismissal. Emilie continued to be a conscientious member of staff. The next summer, matters came to a head.

The entire school was assembled one morning in a room overlooking the garden where Miss Sagee could be seen picking flowers. But when the supervising teacher left the room another Miss Sagee appeared in her chair as if from nowhere. Outside, the 'real' Emilie could still be clearly seen gathering flowers, although her movements appeared to be sluggish, as if her vitality had drained away. Two of the more inquisitive girls took the opportunity to step forward and gingerly touch the double in the chair. To one it felt like muslin, but not entirely solid. Another girl passed right through the apparition by walking between the table and the chair. The *doppelgänger* remained still and lifeless. Moments later it faded and the girls observed that the real Emilie became herself again, moving among the flower beds with some purpose.

The girls quizzed Miss Sagee at the first opportunity, but all she could remember was that when she had seen the teacher leave the room she had wished that she could have been there to supervise the class until their teacher returned. Evidently, her thoughts had preceded her.

Unfortunately for Miss Sagee and the school this incident was not the last. Thirty fee-paying pupils were removed by their concerned parents over the following 18 months after stories about the phenomenon became the prime subject of the girls' letters home. Reluctantly, the headmistress was finally forced to let Miss Sagee go. Emilie was saddened but not surprised. It was the nineteenth position she had been forced to leave in her 16-year career.

THE ABSENT MP

Politicians are not usually considered to be imaginative individuals and so the British newspapers made the most of an incident in 1905 in which the living apparition of British MP Sir Frederick Carne Rasch appeared in the House of Commons at the same moment that his body lay in bed suffering from influenza. Sir Frederick had been so anxious to attend the debate that he had obviously willed himself to appear, but his concentration must have weakened because he vanished before the vote was taken. When he returned to Parliament a few days later MPs delighted in prodding him to see if he was really there in the flesh.

PHANTOM FORERUNNERS

Bi-location may be uncommon, but it is not inconceivable that the mind might be capable of disassociation to such a degree that it enables the essence of a person to appear elsewhere. However, the phenomenon known as the 'phantom forerunner' is far more difficult to explain. The best known example is that of businessman Erkson Gorique who visited Norway in July 1955 for the first time in his life. Or was it?

When Erkson checked into his hotel the clerk greeted him like a valued customer. 'It's good to have you back, Mr Gorique,' said the clerk. 'But I've never been here before,' Gorique replied. 'You must have mistaken me for someone else.' The clerk was certain he was not mistaken. 'But sir, don't you remember? Just a few months ago you dropped in to make a reservation and said you'd be along about this time in the summer. Your name is unusual. That's why I remembered it.' Erkson assured the clerk that this was his first visit to the country. The next day he went to introduce himself to his first potential client, a wholesaler named Olsen, and again he was greeted like a valued customer. 'Ah, Mr Gorique. I'm glad to see you again. Your last visit was much too short.' Erkson was confused and explained what had happened to him at the hotel. To his surprise, Olsen just smiled. 'This is not so unusual here in Norway,' he said. 'In fact, it happens so often we have a name for it. We call it the *vardoger*, or forerunner.'

The phantom forerunner is not exclusively a Norwegian phenomenon, but the country has such an uncommonly high occurrence of such incidents that it has given rise to the greeting, 'Is that you or your *vardoger*?'

In England such apparitions have traditionally been filed away as just another inexplicable ghost story. In 1882, Dr George Wyld reported an incident involving a close acquaintance, Miss Jackson. She had been distributing food to the poor in the neighbourhood on a bitterly cold day when she had a sudden urge to return home to warm herself by the kitchen stove. At that moment her two maids were sitting in the kitchen and observed the door knob turning and the door open revealing a very lifelike Miss Jackson. Startled at their employer's early return they jumped to their feet and watched as she walked to the stove, took off her green kid gloves and warmed her hands. Then vanished. The maids ran to Miss Jackson's mother and described what they had seen, but the old woman assured them that her daughter did not own a pair of green gloves, so they must have imagined it. Half an hour later the lady herself arrived, walked to the kitchen stove, removed her green kid gloves and warmed her hands.

GETTING AHEAD OF THEMSELVES

Frederick Myers' *Phantasms of the Living* includes a case of a multiple forerunner, complete with a horse and carriage.

The Reverend W. Mountford of Boston was visiting a friend when he looked out of the dining room window and saw a carriage approaching the rear of the house. 'Your guests have arrived,' said Mountford, whereupon his host joined him at the window. Both men observed the carriage turn the corner as if it was going to the entrance. But no one rang the door bell and the servants did not announce the arrival of their visitors. Instead, the host's niece entered looking rather flustered having walked all the way from her home, and informed Mountford and his host that her parents had just passed her without acknowledging her or offering her a lift. Ten minutes later the real carriage arrived with the host's brother and his wife. They denied all knowledge of having passed their daughter en route.

Such incidents are not, however, confined to the nineteenth century. As recently as 1980 an Austrian woman, Hilda Saxer, reported seeing a grey Audi belonging to her sister's fiancé, Johann Hofer, passing by at 11.30pm as she left the restaurant where she worked. She waved and the driver, whom she saw clearly and recognized as Johann, smiled and waved back. As she watched the car disappear into the distance the incident struck her as odd because Johann had left the restaurant half an hour earlier.

An hour later Johann's father heard his son's car pull into the driveway and the characteristic sound of the engine as the young man manoeuvred into his parking place. But he did not hear Johann enter the house. The next morning the father was worried when his son did not join him for breakfast. The radio had reported a tunnel collapse on the route Johann had taken on his way home from the restaurant at 11.30pm that same night. The father had heard the car in the drive and assumed his son must have left early that morning. It was only days later that rescuers found the wreckage of the car and its driver, crushed beneath tons of rubble.

THOUGHT FORMS

Science is slowly and reluctantly beginning to acknowledge that the human mind has the power to project a self-image to another location or to separate spirit and body at will. But what is not generally known, even among the earlier pioneers of parapsychology, is the capacity of the human mind to create and sustain images, or thought forms, which can be empowered with a life of their own. Such forms are known as tulpas in the Tibetan esoteric tradition and Golem in the Jewish magical tradition where their creation is considered one of the advanced techniques which must be mastered by initiates before they can become adepts.

The only known record describing the creation of one of these man-made ghosts is the account written by the French mystic and adventurer Alexandra David-Neel (1868–1969) who became the first female lama and the only outsider to be initiated into the secret doctrine of Tibetan Buddhism.

'Besides having had the opportunities of seeing thought-forms, my habitual incredulity led me to make experiments for myself, and my efforts were attended with some success . . . I chose for my experiment a most insignificant character: a monk short and fat, of an innocent and jolly type.

I shut myself in tsams (meditative seclusion) and pro-ceeded to perform the prescribed concentration of *thought and other rites. After a few months the phantom monk was formed. His form grew gradually 'fixed' and life-like. He became a kind of guest, living in my apartment. I then broke my seclusion and started for a tour, with my servants and tents.*

The monk included himself in the party. Though I lived in the open, riding on horseback for miles each day, the illusion persisted. I saw the fat trapa *(novice monk), now and then it was not necessary for me to think of him to make him appear. The phantom performed various actions of the kind that are natural to travellers and that I had not commanded. For instance, he walked, stopped, looked around him. The illusion was mostly visual, but sometimes I felt as if a robe was lightly rubbing against me and once a hand seemed to touch my shoulder.*

The features which I had imagined when building my phantom, gradually underwent a change. The fat, chubby-cheeked fellow grew leaner, his face assumed a vaguely mocking, sly malignant look. He became more troublesome and bold. In brief, he escaped my control.

Once, a herdsman who brought me a present of butter
saw the tulpa in my tent and took it for a live lama. I
ought to have let the phenomenon follow its course,
but the presence of that unwanted companion began
to prove trying to my nerves; it turned into a 'day-
nightmare'. Moreover, I was ... [going] to Lahsa ... so
I decided to dissolve the phantom. I succeeded, but only
after six months of hard struggle. My mind-creature was
tenacious of life.'

CRISIS APPARITIONS

Sailors have always been notoriously fond of a good
ghost story, but the tale told by seaman Robert Bruce to
the nineteenth-century paranormal researcher Robert
Dale Owen is both singular and significant as it is one
of the earliest recorded examples of a crisis apparition,
a phenomenon which is more common than one might
imagine.

In 1828, Bruce was the first mate aboard a cargo ship

ploughing through the icy waters off the Canadian coast. During the voyage he entered the captain's cabin to find a stranger bent over a slate, writing intensely and in great haste. The figure appeared solid, but there was an other-worldly aspect to him and a grave expression on his face which unnerved Bruce. When the stranger raised his head and looked at him, Bruce fled fearing that the presence of the phantom foretold disaster for all on board. He found the skipper on deck and persuaded him to return to the cabin. 'I never was a believer in ghosts,' said Bruce as they made their way below deck, 'but if the truth must be told sir, I'd rather not face it alone.' But when they entered the cabin it was empty. However, they found the slate and on it were scrawled the words 'Steer to the nor'west'.

At first the skipper suspected that the crew were playing a practical joke, so he ordered them all to copy the message. After comparing their handwriting with the original he had to admit he could not identify the culprit. A search of the entire ship failed to find any stowaways, leaving the captain with an unusual dilemma: to ignore the message and risk having the lives of untold lost souls on his conscience, or change his course and risk being thought of as a superstitious old fool in the eyes of the crew. He chose to change course.

Fortunately, he had made the right decision. Within hours they came upon a stricken vessel that had been critically damaged by an iceberg. There were only minutes to save the passengers and crew before it sank beneath the waves. Bruce watched with grim satisfaction and relief as the survivors were brought aboard, but then he saw something which haunted him to his dying day. He came face to face with the stranger he had seen scrawling the message earlier that day in the captain's cabin.

After the man had recovered sufficiently to be questioned, Bruce and the captain asked him to copy the message on the slate. They compared the two sets of handwriting. There was no question about it – they were identical. Initially, the 'stranger' couldn't account for his early presence on the ship until he recalled a dream that he had had about the same time that Bruce had seen his 'ghost' in the captain's cabin. After falling asleep from exhaustion he had dreamt that he was aboard a ship that was coming to rescue him and his fellow survivors. He told the others of his dream to reassure them that help was on its way and he even described the rescue ship, all of which proved correct in every detail. The captain of the wrecked ship confirmed his story. 'He described her appearance and rig,' he told their rescuers, 'and to our utter astonishment, when your vessel hove in sight, she corresponded exactly to his description of her.'

ESCAPING WORLDLY BONDS

One of the most revealing examples of an out-of-body experience happens to be one of the first to be published in a respected medical journal, the *St Louis Medical and Surgical Journal*, in February 1890. It is also of great interest because the subject was a doctor who understood what was happening to him and was able to observe his own 'death' with clinical detachment.

Dr A.S. Wiltse of Kansas contracted typhoid fever in the summer of 1889. After saying his last goodbyes to his family, he lapsed into unconsciousness. But although his body exhibited no signs of life – neither pulse nor heartbeat – inside his own dead body Dr Wiltse was fully conscious and observing the grieving around him with a curious detachment. It was as if he had reverted to pure consciousness, acutely alert but unemotional. 'I learned that the epidermis [skin] was the outside boundary of the ultimate tissues, so to speak, of the soul.' He then felt a gentle swaying and a separation which he compared to the snapping of tiny cords. In another moment he was looking out from his skull . 'As I emerged from the head I floated up and down . . . like a soap bubble . . . until I at last broke loose from the body and fell lightly to the floor, where I slowly rose and expanded into the full stature of a man.' At this point he felt embarrassed to discover that there were two women in the room, but then he realized that he was not naked but clothed – merely by wishing to be so.

Here, perhaps, is a crucial clue as to why ghosts appear in the form that they do, often younger and in better health than when their physical shell expired. Dr Wiltse had left his body as a shapeless, colourless bubble of etheric energy, but as soon as he became aware of his surroundings he was able to assume a more acceptable form and projected his own self-image which would have been his ideal self. It was then that he passed straight through another man in the room before he realized what he was doing. He saw the funny side of the situation, which may have been partly due to the relief in finding himself very much alive in this new reality. He intuitively 'knew' that this was his natural state, his true self. His personality was the same after death as it had been in life, but he had left behind his fears and his sense of identity. He no longer identified with the body on the bed. He was no longer concerned with what happened to it. That was the part of him that felt pain, disappointment, regrets. This 'greater self' was beyond those petty, worldly concerns. If this was 'death', it was nothing more than slipping off a worn out coat or walking through an open door into the world outside.

He was becoming accustomed to his new 'body' and was eager to explore. As he passed through the door he looked back and saw a thin elasticated web-like cord connecting him to the lifeless body on the bed, the etheric equivalent of the umbilical cord. So long as he remained attached by this cord he knew he could return to his body at will. He was not dead, as he had originally thought, but merely temporarily detached – a living ghost. He walked along a road idly wondering where the other 'dead' people might be and if this is all there was to being dead. Suddenly he lost consciousness and when he next became aware of where he was he found himself in an unfamiliar landscape over which hung a black cloud. Ahead he saw three enormous rocks which an inner voice informed him was the boundary to the 'eternal world'. At this point he intuitively knew that this was as far as he would be permitted to go on this occasion and with that realization he woke up – much to the surprise of his doctor. Dr Wiltse had been clinically dead for four hours, but had suffered no permanent brain damage or other ill effects, contrary to the laws of medical science. A religious man might call this a miracle, but in the years that followed it became increasingly evident that such out-of-body experiences have been shared by hundreds of thousands of people around the world and that they are neither miraculous nor supernatural. They are perfectly natural.

A GHOST IN THE MIRROR

Vermont housewife Caroline Larsen considered herself an unremarkable person, preoccupied with social conventions, her standing in the community and her obligations as the dutiful middle-class wife of an amateur musician. But, one autumn evening in 1910, she discovered her true self as she went one step further than Dr Wiltse had done during a strikingly similar out-of-body experience.

As Mrs Larsen lay in bed listening to her husband and his friends practising a Beethoven string quartet she began to feel a creeping sense of foreboding. No matter how hard she tried to focus on the soothing strains of the music she was unable to relax and throw off her apprehension.

'The overpowering oppression deepened and soon numbness crept over me until every muscle became paralyzed . . . finally everything became a blank. The next thing I knew was that I, I myself, was standing on the floor beside my bed looking down attentively on my own physical body lying in it.'

She observed that her room was unchanged. But after proceeding down the hall into the bathroom she instinctively reached for the light switch and was surprised that she couldn't connect with it. It was then that she noticed that the room was illuminated by a softer light emanating from her own body.

'Looking in to the mirror I became aware for the first time of the astonishing transformation I had undergone. Instead of seeing a middle-aged woman, I beheld the figure of a girl about 18 years of age. I recognised the form and features of my girlhood. But I was now infinitely more beautiful. My face appeared as if it were chiselled out of the finest alabaster and it seemed transparent, as did my arms and hands when I raised them to touch my hair . . . But they were not entirely translucent for in the centre of the arms and hands and fingers there was a darker, more compact substance, as in x-ray photographs. My eyes, quite strong in the physical body, were piercingly keen now . . . my hair, no longer grey, was now, as in my youth, dark brown and it fell in waves over my shoulders and down my back. And, to my delight, I was dressed in the loveliest white shining garment imaginable – a sleeveless one-piece dress, cut low at the neck and reaching almost to the ankles.'

She then had the idea to walk down the stairs and surprise her husband and his friends in her new youthful form.

'Turning away from the mirror I walked out into the hall, enjoying in anticipation the success of my plan, I stepped on gaily. I revelled in the feeling of bodily lightness . . . I moved with the freedom of thought.

'[But] just as I came to the little platform which divides the stairway into two flights I saw, standing before me, a woman spirit in shining clothes with arms outstretched and with forefinger pointing upwards . . . she spoke to me sternly, "Where are you going? Go back to your body!"

. . . I knew instinctively – that from this spirit's command and authority there was no appeal.'

Returning to her room she found her body on the bed, just as 'still and lifeless' as she had left it.

'I viewed it with feelings of loathing and disappointment. I knew that I would soon have to enter it again, no matter how ugly it seemed to me or how much I shrank from it. In another instant I had again joined with my *physical form. With a gasp and a start, I woke up in it.'*

The image she describes may sound like an aging person's fantasy, but the deceased often appear as their younger selves. In effect, they are so used to having a physical body that they cannot imagine themselves without one and so manifest as their ideal self-image.

PROJECTING HIS OWN GHOST

Most of the hundreds of thousands of out-of-body experiences and near-death experiences that have been recorded involve the involuntary separation of the spirit from the body at a moment of crisis or physical danger or during an altered state of consciousness. But there are a surprising number of incidents in which the astral traveller has consciously projected their spirit double to another location.

Sylvan Joseph Muldoon, the son of a spiritualist in Clinton, Iowa, claimed to have acquired the ability to leave his body at will. He had enjoyed dozens of liberating out-of-body experiences since the age of 12, but it was not until 10 years later, in 1925, that he had the confirmation that what he was experiencing was more than a lucid dream.

During this excursion he found himself propelled at incredible speed to an unfamiliar farmhouse somewhere in the same rural region where he lived. There he observed four people passing a pleasant evening, including an attractive young girl who was engaged in sewing a black dress. They seemed unaware of his presence so he wandered around the room noting the furnishings and ornaments until it occurred to him that he had no business being there. With that thought he returned to his body. It was more than a month later that Muldoon happened to see the same girl in town and asked her where she lived. She thought he was prying or being 'fresh' and told him to mind his own business, but when he described her home in astonishing detail and told her how he knew this, she confirmed everything that he had seen.

INDUCING AN OUT-OF-BODY EXPERIENCE

If you wish to prove the existence of the etheric body for yourself, this exercise can be used to trigger an OBE. Although such experiences occur naturally and should never be forced, this safe and simple technique for the gradual separation of spirit and body has been practised by mystics through the centuries. However, it needs to be stressed that such techniques should never be attempted while under the influence of alcohol or drugs of any kind. Nor should they be attempted by anyone who has, or is currently suffering from, any form of psychological disturbance, abnormal grief or trauma. If in doubt you should seek medical advice before attempting any of these techniques.

1. Lie on your back on the floor, an exercise mat or bed and ensure you support your neck with a small pillow or cushion. Your arms should be loose by your side and not crossed over on your chest or stomach. Your legs must be straight.

2. Establish a steady rhythm of breathing and, as you dissolve deeper into relaxation, repeat a phrase that relaxes you and induces a sense of security, such as 'calm and centred' or 'I am perfect and at peace'.

3. After a few minutes you may sense a warming of the solar plexus centre beneath your navel. Visualize a soft pulsing light in your abdomen as this energy centre softens, loosening the silver umbilical cord of etheric energy which connects your spirit double to your physical shell. Feel it unwinding as you sink deeper and deeper into a detached state. As you do so you will begin to lose the sense of the weight and solidity of your body. You become lighter with every breath.

4. Now visualize your breath forming a cushion of air under your back until you feel that you can float away like a cloud on the breeze. Feel yourself rising a few inches above your body and then being drawn back by the silver cord as you enjoy exercising control over your new found ability. You are safe and in control at all times. You only have to wish to return to your body and you will do so in an instant.

5. Transfer your awareness to this 'real you' by visualizing the room from a new perspective as if you were standing and walking around. Then imagine yourself looking down on your physical body from the ceiling – you may find you have 'popped out' and are now free to explore. If not, visualize yourself exploring the room in your spirit body and your awareness will be transferred to it. Until you are comfortable being outside your body it would be advisable to stay within the confines of your own home, but as soon as you feel confident you can begin to explore the neighbourhood and beyond.

• Be patient and persistent. It may take several attempts to make the breakthrough. You will know that you are out of the body and not dreaming because you will experience a euphoria as you realize you have liberated the real you. If you want to obtain absolute proof of this you can try the following experiment. However, if you do so, make sure your partner will treat it seriously or you risk having your confidence undermined.

• Remember: You are under no obligation to try this exercise. Out-of-body experiences are a natural phenomenon and should never be forced. If you feel uncomfortable for any reason do not attempt this exercise or you risk instilling fear in your self which may inhibit your development.

THE ASTRAL VISIT

To obtain a truly objective result in this experiment you will need the co-operation of a friend whom you can trust to take the exercise seriously. The object of the exercise is to obtain conclusive proof of your ability to visit them at will in your etheric body.

To do this ask your friend to put a book of their choice on a chair in their bedroom with the cover face up. They must not tell you what they are going to place there and they should not decide which book to use until shortly beforehand, otherwise it is possible that you will obtain the answer by telepathy instead. Decide on a specific time for the experiment so that your partner can note any changes that may occur in the atmosphere and can be alert at the allotted time.

Again, be patient. It may take several attempts to make the breakthrough.

A MESSAGE FROM THE OTHER SIDE

Near-death experiences typically involve an individual leaving their body, passing through a tunnel of light into a more vibrant reality and then returning to their body with a renewed appetite for life. But the experience of Dr Karl Novotny was different in one significant respect. He did not return. Instead he described the process of dying from the other side using the services of a medium. Such anecdotal evidence usually has the sceptics shrieking with derision, but the case of Dr Novotny is notable for several reasons.

Two days prior to his death in Easter 1965, Novotny's friend, Grete Schroeder, dreamt that he appeared before her to announce his death. Neither Schroeder nor Novotny were interested in psychic phenomena – in fact quite the reverse. Novotny was a pupil of the celebrated psychologist Arthur Adler and was inclined to explain every phenomenon in terms of the untapped powers of the unconscious. When Novotny died as 'he' had predicted, Grete felt compelled to consult a medium rather than risk becoming prey to doubts for the rest of her life. She evidently chose a reputable psychic because not only did the details of his death – as relayed by the medium – tally with the facts, she also transcribed what he told her in a script which Grete recognized as Novotny's own handwriting even though the medium had never met him. The description of his dying moments is uncannily similar to that related by thousands of other individuals from around the world who have had a near-death experience and it is worth quoting for comparison.

'I turned back to my companions and found myself looking down at my own body on the ground. My friends were in despair, calling for a doctor, and trying to get a car to take me home. But I was well and felt no pains. I couldn't understand what had happened. I bent down and felt the heart of the body lying on the ground. Yes – it had ceased to beat – I was dead. But I was still alive! I spoke to my friends, but they neither saw me nor answered me . . .

And then there was my dog, who kept whining pitifully, unable to decide to which of me he should go, for he saw me in two places at once, standing up and lying down on the ground.

When all the formalities were concluded and my body had been put in a coffin, I realised that I must be dead.

*But I wouldn't acknowledge the fact; for, like my teacher
Arthur Adler, I did not believe in after-life.'*

Novotny then visited his friend Grete and found her
sitting alone and immersed in grief, but again his
attempts to communicate were fruitless. She did not
seem aware of his presence and did not respond when
he spoke to her.

*'It was no use. I had to recognise the truth. When finally I
did so I saw my dear mother coming to meet me with open
arms, telling me that I had passed into the next world –
not in words, of course, since these only belong to the earth.
Even so, I couldn't credit her statement and thought I must
be dreaming. This belief continued for a long time. I fought
against the truth and was most unhappy . . .'*

THE PSYCHOLOGIST AND THE SPIRIT

Dutch psychologist Elleke Van Kraalingen was a

pragmatic, scientifically-minded woman who prided herself on having a healthy scepticism towards the supernatural. The demands of her professional life meant that she was totally grounded in the here and now and had no desire to probe the secrets of life and death. That was until she witnessed the sudden and violent death of her fiancé, Hermod, in a hit and run accident. In her autobiography, *Beyond the Boundary of Life and Death*, Elleke describes how she was awoken to the reality of the soul's survival after death as she knelt over his body and sensed a 'tearing apart' of the subtle bond between them, as it was severed. She then 'saw' his soul leave his body as a mist and sensed his presence standing behind her during her desperate efforts to revive him. While the emotional part of her was in turmoil, the intellectual aspect of her being calmly reassured her that he was well. After the ambulance had taken his body, Elleke walked back to their hotel, all the while sensing that Hermod was beside her holding her hand.

That evening he materialized in their room, sitting on

the edge of her bed as solid as he had been 24 hours earlier. Having been trained to dismiss everything connected with the paranormal as irrational and the creation of a troubled mind, Elleke instinctively denied what she was seeing as a hallucination brought on by grief. She covered her eyes and affirmed that she was imagining it, but when she looked again he was still there, as large as life. It was at this point that she heard him speak inside her head in a quiet consoling tone that was quite distinct from her own thoughts. 'I'm still here,' he told her. 'There is no death, there is no time, there's only reality.'

He was not the only discarnate spirit in the room. Elleke sensed the presence of others that she felt were there to help his transition from this world to the next. When he and his companions had gone she wrote everything down so that she could analyze her thought processes at a later date when she was not so emotionally involved. She hoped this would help her discover the cause of her delusion. Even at this point Elleke was convinced that what she had seen was a projection of her own internal turmoil. Perhaps this was a replay of her memories of Hermod triggered automatically as a result of an emotional crisis, like a drowning person who sees their life replayed in their mind like a film.

But the next day Hermod reappeared again, as solid as he was when he was alive. Elleke was the only person who could see him, presumably because she perceived him with the eyes of the spirit – the inner eye or third eye of psychic sight. That day he remained with her as she sleepwalked through the traumatic process of identifying his body and dealing with the police. It was only after the funeral that she sensed him withdraw, leaving her to cope with life alone.

And then an extraordinary thing happened. Several days later, while Elleke was meditating in an attempt to calm and centre herself, he reappeared and drew her out of her body. In this state she was able to look down at her physical self sitting cross-legged on the floor and view the world with a detachment she could not have attained while in her body. She described this state as liberating and more vibrantly real than what she had previously considered to be reality. When they embraced she felt totally absorbed in the core of his being, not merely comforted or connected as she had done when they were in their physical bodies. She sensed that it was only when they were out of body that they could truly know each other. Soon she felt drained and snapped back into her physical shell – either the effort of remaining out of the body for a long period was too much for her, or perhaps he was unintentionally draining her of her life force in order to remain at this level.

Over the following months, Hermod materialized and took her on an astral tour of other realms or realities where discarnate beings communicated with them by thought alone. In these realms the dead created their own heaven and hell according to their expectations and beliefs. Those who could not accept their own death remained earthbound, reliving the most significant experiences of their lives as if in a recurring dream and visible to the living as ghosts.

PSYCHOLOGY AND THE PARANORMAL

Mainstream science and orthodox religion are considered custodians of good sense by those who believe in the infallibility of science or the absolute truth of the Bible. But both fields have their share of individualists who are not as rigid in their thinking as one might suspect.

Carl Jung (1875–1961), the founding father of analytical psychology, was fiercely proud of his reputation as a pioneer of the new science, but in private he continually wrestled to reconcile psychology and the paranormal. He wrote:

'In the end the only events in my life worth telling are those when the imperishable world irrupted into this transitory one. That is why I speak chiefly of inner experiences, among which I include my dreams and visions. These form the prima materia of my scientific work. They were the fiery magma out of which the stone that had to be worked was crystallised.'

Jung's maternal grandfather was the vicar of Kesswil, Switzerland, and was said to be blessed with 'second sight'. His family blithely accepted that he conversed with the dead in defiance of church edicts. As Jung wrote:

> *'My mother often told me how she had to sit behind him while he wrote his sermons because he could not bear [to have] ghosts pass behind him while he was studying. The presence of a living human being at his back frightened them away!'*

His own home life was equally unconventional. As a child Jung was constantly aware of the presence of spirits.

> *'From the door to my mother's room came a frightening influence. At night Mother was strange and mysterious. One night I saw coming from her door a faintly luminous indefinite figure whose head detached itself from the neck and floated along in front of it, in the air like a little moon.'*

In his youth Jung witnessed at first hand phenomena during séances held by his 15-year-old cousin, Helene Preiswerk, who had developed mediumistic powers. Helene channelled a number of dead relatives who spoke in their own distinctive voices and passed on personal details which the young 'Helly' could not have known about. Jung was particularly struck by the change in his cousin's manner when she went into a trance. She exhibited a maturity and breadth of knowledge that was at odds with her provincial frivolous nature. But although Jung was initially convinced that her abilities were genuine, he later felt obliged to find a rational explanation when writing up the case for his inaugural dissertation. It was a classic example of multiple personality, he concluded, brought on by hysteria and sexual repression. Although such a diagnosis might account for a good number of fraudulent mediums, Jung also knew that he risked being discredited as a serious man of science if he subscribed to the spiritualist creed. Privately, however, he remained a firm believer in the paranormal and was intolerant of those, like Freud, who scoffed at such things on principle.

'I wondered at the sureness with which they could assert that things like ghosts and table turning were impossible and therefore fraudulent, and on the other hand, at the evidently anxious nature of their defensiveness. For myself I found such possibilities extremely interesting and attractive. They added another dimension to my life; the world gained depth and background.'

In his autobiography, *Memories, Dreams, Reflections,* Jung describes his own paranormal experiences including the plague of poltergeist activity with which his home was besieged in the summer of 1916.

'The house was filled as if it was crammed full of spirits and the air was so thick it was scarcely possible to breathe . . . My eldest daughter saw a white figure pass through her room. My second daughter, independently

> *... related that twice in the night her blanket had been snatched away ...'*

Over three successive evenings he channelled a series of messages from discarnate spirits which formed the basis of Seven Sermons From The Dead, a series of Hermetic discourses on the nature of God, and Good and Evil in a contrived archaic style. It was only when he had completed this task that the spirits withdrew and the 'haunting' ceased. Jung dismissed the attendant poltergeist activity as 'exteriorization phenomena', meaning that he interpreted it as his own unconscious demanding his attention to the coming task.

> *'It has taken me virtually forty-five years to distil within the vessel of my scientific work the things I experienced and wrote down at that time ... The years when I was pursuing my inner images were the most important in my life – in them everything essential was decided. It all began then; the later details are only supplements and*

clarifications of the material that burst forth from the unconscious, and at first swamped me. It was the prima materia for a lifetime's work.'

THE HAUNTED COTTAGE

Despite a lifetime of witnessing paranormal phenomena at first hand, Jung still felt the need to hedge his bets. In 1919, he wrote a paper for the SPR entitled 'The Psychological Foundation of Belief in Spirits' in which he stated that such phenomena can be dismissed as projections of the unconscious mind. The following year the spirits had their revenge.

In 1920, Jung arrived in Britain on a lecture tour and stayed in a country cottage so that he could be alone. The rent was nominal, but either Jung did not suspect that this might be because the place was haunted, or he didn't attach any importance to it. On the first weekend he was disturbed by a rancid odour permeating the bedroom, although there was no obvious source of the smell. The following weekend, the smell returned accompanied by a rustling noise as if an animal was exploring the room, or perhaps a woman in a crinoline dress was brushing against the walls. On the third weekend, his work was interrupted by inexplicable rapping sounds. Again, there was no obvious source for these noises. On the fifth weekend, he was startled to wake up next to the ghost of an old woman, her face partly dissolved as if pressed into a pillow.

The locals subsequently confirmed that the cottage was inhabited by a malevolent spirit and that is why they refused to stay there after dusk. But Jung was not so easily disturbed. He invited the friend who had rented the cottage for him to spend the night, and the man was so terrified when he heard phantom footsteps that he abandoned his bed after just a few hours and spent the rest of the night sleeping in the garden with a shotgun by his side. Jung recollected, 'It gave me considerable satisfaction after my colleague had laughed so loudly at my fear of ghosts.'

His own attitude to such phenomena remained ambiguous despite his extraordinary experiences. He was clearly impressed with the 'performance' of respected medium Rudi Schneider (whose talents were detailed in Thomas Mann's essay *An Experience With The Occult*) although he could not bring himself to credit his cousin Helly with the same abilities. For all his insights into the human mind, Jung was forced to admit that he did not have an explanation for these phenomena. 'Either there are physical processes which cause psychic happenings, or there is a pre-existent psyche which organises matter.'

If he expected his mentor Sigmund Freud to resolve the question he was to be disappointed. In one memorable episode, Jung and Freud were arguing about the existence of poltergeists when a loud report shook a nearby bookcase. Freud insisted it was merely the furniture settling, even though the weather was mild and could not have caused the wood to contract or expand. But Jung had felt heat building up in his solar plexus from his frustration at being treated like a wilful student of the great man and he was certain that he himself was the source of the kinetic activity. 'There will be another report in a moment,' he predicted and, sure enough, there was.

OUT OF THIS WORLD

Paranormal phenomena and psychic experiences pursued Jung all through his life. Then, in April 1944, at the age of 68, he had an out-of-body experience that was to have a profound effect on his perception of the world and which turned his concept of reality on its head. The extracts below are from his autobiography, *Memories, Dreams, Reflections* (1961):

'It seemed to me that I was high up in space. Far below I saw the globe of the earth, bathed in a gloriously blue light. I saw the deep blue sea and the continents. Far below my feet lay Ceylon, and in the distance ahead of me the subcontinent of India. My field of vision did not include the whole earth, but its global shape was plainly

*distinguishable and its outlines shone with a silvery
gleam through that wonderful blue light . . . I knew that
I was on the point of departing from the earth.*

*Later I discovered how high in space one would have
to be to have so extensive a view – approximately a
thousand miles! The sight of the earth from this height
was the most glorious thing I had ever seen . . . I myself
was floating in space.'*

At this point Jung felt that he was stripped down to the
essence of his being.

*' . . . everything I aimed at or wished for or thought, the
whole phantasmagoria of earthly existence, fell away or
was stripped from me – an extremely painful process.
Nevertheless something remained; it was as if I now
carried along with me everything I had ever experienced
or done, everything that had happened around me . . .
This experience gave me a feeling of extreme poverty,
but at the same time of great fullness. There was no*

longer anything I wanted or desired. I existed in an objective form; I was what I had been and lived. At first the sense of annihilation predominated, of having been stripped or pillaged; but suddenly that became of no consequence. Everything seemed to be past.'

While he was contemplating the significance of this greater reality he became aware of another presence, that of his doctor who appeared before Jung in his 'primal form'.

'. . . a mute exchange of thought took place between us. The doctor had been delegated by the earth to deliver a message to me, to tell me that there was a protest against my going away. I had no right to leave the earth and must return. The moment I heard that, the vision ceased.

I was profoundly disappointed, for now it all seemed to have been for nothing. The painful process of defoliation had been in vain . . . Life and the whole world struck me as a prison, and it bothered me beyond measure that I should again be finding all that quite in order. I had been so glad to shed it all . . . I felt violent resistance to my doctor because he had brought me back to life. At the same time, I was worried about him. "His life is in danger, for heaven's sake! He has appeared to me in his primal form! When anybody attains this form it means he is going to die, for already he belongs to the 'greater company'." Suddenly the terrifying thought came to me that the doctor would have to die in my stead. I tried my best to talk to him about it, but he did not understand me. Then I became angry with him.

In actual fact I was his last patient. On April 4, 1944 . . . I was allowed to sit up on the edge of my bed for the first time since the beginning of my illness, and on this same day the doctor took to his bed and did not leave it again. I heard that he was having intermittent attacks of fever. Soon afterward he died of septicemia . . .

It was not a product of imagination. The visions and experiences were utterly real; there was nothing subjective about them; they all had a quality of absolute objectivity.'

In *Synchronicity* (1952), Jung cites the case of a woman patient who left her body during childbirth and observed the medical procedures used to revive her which she described to her nurse after recovering consciousness. She was correct in every detail. The most astonishing part was her discovery that while in her astral body she possessed perceptions independent of her physical senses. At the same moment that she was watching the frantic efforts of the medical staff, she was also aware of a vivid pastoral landscape 'behind' her which she knew to be the 'other world'. By a conscious effort of will she remained focused on the doctors and nurses for fear that she might be tempted by the bliss of the other world to drift into it and not return.

CRISIS OF FAITH

Eminent theological scholar Canon J.B. Phillips regarded himself as a conscientious servant of the Church of the England with an unshakable belief in the articles of his faith. These denied the existence of apparitions other than the Holy Ghost, yet Canon Phillips was convinced that he had had a visitation from C.S. Lewis, the recently deceased Christian philosopher and author of the *Narnia* novels, in late November 1963. He confided the details of his encounter in his journal.

'Let me say at once that I am incredulous by nature and as unsuperstitious as they come. I have never bothered about . . . any of the current superstitions which may occupy the human heart in the absence of faith . . . But the late C.S. Lewis, whom I did not know very well and had only seen in the flesh once, but with whom I had corresponded a fair amount, gave me an unusual experience. A few days after his death, while I was watching television, he 'appeared' sitting in a chair a few feet from me, and spoke a few words which were particularly relevant to the difficult circumstances through which I was passing. He was ruddier in complexion than ever, grinning all over his face, and, *as the saying has it, positively glowing with health. The interesting thing to me was that I had not been thinking about him at all . . .*

A week later, this time when I was in bed reading before going to sleep, he appeared again, even more rosily radiant than before, and repeated to me the same message, which was very important to me at the time. I was a little puzzled by this and mentioned it to a certain saintly bishop who was then living in retirement in Dorset. His reply was, 'My dear J. this sort of thing is happening all the time.'

Canon Phillips' experience is noteworthy for several reasons. The first being that he was not a believer in spirits – in fact he was effectively under orders to deny their existence and had much to lose by admitting to what he had seen. Secondly, he saw the same apparition on two separate occasions which would seem to rule out the possibility that they were hypnagogic hallucinations (the hypnagogic state is that state between being awake and falling asleep), or waking dreams caused by fatigue or stress. Thirdly, Lewis' 'ghost' spoke and the advice he gave was relevant to Canon Phillips' situation. Furthermore, on the one occasion when Phillips had met Lewis during the latter's lifetime, Lewis was dressed in clerical robes and not the 'well-worn tweeds' in which he appeared after death and which was his customary mode of dress. It was only after Phillips had reported his encounter with the author's ghost that he learnt that Lewis dressed in tweeds. And, lastly, the bishop had evidently heard of such things in the course of his ministrations and took it all in his stride. If it was not a genuine encounter there is only one other explanation, that the apparition was a projection of Canon Phillips' subconscious which took the form of a friend he admired and whose advice he would heed. And that is no less remarkable a phenomenon.

VOICES FROM BEYOND

In the 1920s, Thomas Edison, the prolific American

inventor of the phonograph, the electric lamp, the microphone and the kinetoscope (a forerunner of the movie projector), to name but a few of his creations, admitted to working on a device for contacting the dead. He told *Scientific American* magazine that he believed it was perfectly possible 'to construct an apparatus which will be so delicate that if there are personalities in another existence or sphere who wish to get in touch with us in this existence or sphere, this apparatus will at least give them a better opportunity to express themselves than the tilting tables and raps and Ouija boards and mediums and the other crude methods now purported to be the only means of communication.' Unfortunately, Edison passed over before he could build the contraption, but it now seems that his dream may be closer to being realized than ever before.

The first serious hint that audible communication with the departed may be feasible occurred in June 1959 when Swedish ornithologist Friedrich Jurgenson replayed a recording of birdsong and heard a faint

Norwegian voice discussing the habits of nocturnal birds. At first he thought it must be interference from a local broadcaster or amateur radio enthusiast, but there was no transmitter in the area. Intrigued, he decided to make test recordings at his home to determine whether or not the tape recorder was faulty, but when he listened to the recordings he caught something which chilled him to the marrow. There were voices on the tape that he had not heard when he was recording. They mentioned Jurgenson and his dog by name and correctly predicted an incoming phone call and the name of the caller. In subsequent recording sessions, Jurgenson merely had to turn on the tape for an unspecified length of time and then play it back to hear a babble of faint voices talking among themselves, commenting on him and the other people whom he had invited to be present as witnesses.

As Jurgenson researched the subject he discovered that EVP (Electronic Voice Phenomena) were only one aspect of a wider range of phenomena known collectively as Instrumental Transcommunication (ITC) covering spirit communication through all manner of electronic equipment including radios, telephones, television sets and even computers. Although the more common forms of ITC are indistinct disembodied voices, there have been incidents where the face of the deceased has been seen and positively identified by their relatives breaking through a regular broadcast on a television screen.

RECORDING EVP

If you want to experiment with EVP all you need is a digital recording device such as a mini-disc, DAT recorder or computer and an analogue radio. Cassette recorders are unsuitable as they produce excessive hiss at low volume and also mechanical noise which can cloak the signal. The radio needs to be tuned to a frequency between stations so that a background of white noise is audible for the voices to print through. You will have to be objective when analyzing what you have recorded as it is possible to interpret random interference, 'print-through' from previous recordings, digital 'artefacts' and signals bleeding from adjacent stations as being significant. The potential for misinterpretation is so common that a medical term has been coined to describe it – auditory pareidolia. Consequently, it is necessary to remain detached and foster a healthy scepticism, otherwise you are at risk of reading something significant into what is really only random interference.

THE POPE'S PARAPSYCHOLOGISTS

In 1952, two Italian Catholic priests, Father Ernetti and Father Gemelli, were playing back a tape recording they had made of Gregorian chants when they heard an inaudible whispering in the silence when the singing had stopped. At first they thought it might be radio interference or 'print through', the echo of an earlier recording which occurs when the tape has not been properly erased or the playback heads are misaligned. But when they turned up the volume Father Gemelli recognized the whispering as the voice of his father who had died many years earlier. It was calling Gemelli by his childhood nickname. 'Zucchini, it is clear, don't you know it is I?'

Contact with the dead is forbidden by the Catholic church, but there was no denying what they had heard. So the priests dutifully asked for an audience with Pope Pius XII in Rome and put the problem before him. The Pope's verdict was later published in the Italian Journal Astra.

'Dear Father Gemelli, you really need not worry about this. The existence of this voice is strictly a scientific fact and has nothing to do with spiritism. The recorder is totally objective. It receives and records only sound waves from wherever they come. This experiment may perhaps become the cornerstone for a building for scientific studies which will strengthen people's faith in a hereafter.'

The nonchalant reply stunned the priests, but evidently such phenomena were not news to the Vatican. It later transpired that the Pope's cousin, the Rev Professor Dr Gebhard Frei, co-founder of the Jung Institute, was the President of the International Society for Catholic Parapsychologists and had collaborated with an early pioneer of EVP, Dr Konstantin Raudive, of Germany.

Before his death in October 1967, Frei had gone on record as a staunch advocate of investigating EVP. 'All that I have read and heard forces me to believe that the voices come from transcendental, individual entities. Whether it suits me or not, I have no right to doubt the reality of the voices.' Ironically, as if to validate his own life's work, just a month after his death, the voice of Dr Frei was caught on tape and identified by Professor Peter Hohenwarter of the University of Vienna.

Pope Paul VI, successor to Pope Pius XII, continued the good work, giving his blessing to researches carried out by Swedish film producer Friedrich Jurgenson, who confided to a British voice researcher in the 1960s, 'I have found a sympathetic ear for the Voice Phenomenon in the Vatican. I have won many wonderful friends among the leading figures in the Holy City. Today "the bridge" stands firmly on its foundations.' Presumably, 'the bridge' referred to the work which would reconcile the Church with what it insisted on calling spiritism.

It is believed that the Vatican even agreed to novice priests attending a course in parapsychology under the auspices of Father Andreas Resch. The Church's interest in these phenomena was hardly a secret although it was certainly not widely known. In 1970, the International Society of Catholic Parapsychologists convened in Austria and openly discussed such phenomena as EVP.

Perhaps the Church's most active involvement with such matters was the Pye Recording Studio sessions which took place in England in 1972, funded by the *Sunday Mirror*. The sessions were conducted by theologian Dr Peter Bander, a senior lecturer in Religious and Moral Education at the Cambridge Institute of Education, who was initially hostile to the whole notion of communicating with the dead by any means. Prior to the experiment, Bander declared that it was 'not only far-fetched but outrageous' to even consider the possibility of recording spirit voices. He invited four senior members of the Catholic hierarchy to witness the proceedings in expectation that they would put the matter to rest once and for all. But during the recordings, which were held in a soundproof studio to eliminate the possibility of external interference, it was claimed that the participants heard the voice of a naval officer who had committed suicide two years earlier, a voice that had been recorded by Dr Raudive at an earlier session. The studio's chief engineer, Ken Attwood, conceded, 'I have done everything in my power to break the mystery of the voices without success; the same applies to other experts. I suppose we must learn to accept them.'

When the *Sunday Mirror* refused to publish Bander's conclusions, he published them himself the following year in a book entitled *Breakthrough*. Father Pistone, Superior of the Society of St Paul in England, gave Bander's experiment and his book what sounded like a positive endorsement.

'I do not see anything against the teaching of the Catholic Church in the Voices, they are something extra-ordinary but there is no reason to fear them, nor can I see any danger. The Church realizes that she cannot control the evolution of science. Here we are dealing with a scientific phenomenon; this is progress and the Church is progressive. I am happy to see that representatives of most Churches have adopted the same attitude as we have: we recognize that the subject of the Voice Phenomena stirs the imagination even of those who have always maintained that there could never be any proof or basis for discussion on the question of life after death. This book and the subsequent experiments raise serious doubts, even in the minds of atheists. This alone is a good reason for the Church supporting the experiments. A second reason may be found in the greater flexibility of the Church since Vatican II; we are willing to keep an open mind on all matters which do not contradict Christ's teaching.'

Bander also managed to convert Archbishop H.E.

Cardinale, Apostolic Nuncio to Belgium, who remarked, 'Naturally it is all very mysterious, but we know the voices are there for all to hear them'. The Right Reverend Monsignor, Professor C. Pfleger added, 'Facts have made us realize that between death and resurrection, there is another realm of post-mortal existence. Christian theology has little to say about this realm.'

Following the publicity surrounding the Pye sessions, the Vatican commissioned Swiss theologian Father Leo Schmid to embark on further research. Schmid went on to amass over 10,000 recordings which were transcribed and edited in his posthumously published book *When the Dead Speak* (1976). More recently, Vatican spokesman Father Gino Concetti told the papal newspaper *Osservatore Romano*:

'According to the modern catechism, God allows our dear departed persons who live in an ultra-terrestrial dimension, to send messages to guide us in certain difficult moments of our lives. The Church has decided

not to forbid any more the dialogue with the deceased with the condition that these contacts are carried out with a serious religious and scientific purpose.'

It would appear that the Church has made its peace with the dead.

CHAPTER 4

Talking to the dead

The most convincing evidence of the
soul's survival after death comes from
psychic mediums who act as a channel
between the living and the dead.

MOST PEOPLE have never seen a ghost, but that does not mean that ghosts do not exist. There is considerable experiential evidence that discarnate spirits do exist, but in an alternate reality to our own. This is a non-physical dimension of which we are not conscious because our perception of this greater reality is limited by our five physical senses.

SCIENCE AND THE SPIRIT WORLD

We operate at the lowest frequency of existence on the densest level, the physical plane. Naturally, we tend to believe that what we perceive is real and that anything that we cannot touch, taste, see, smell or hear does not exist. Our world appears solid but, as science has recently discovered, this is an illusion created by the comparatively low processing power of the human brain which cannot see the spaces that exist between matter at the subatomic level. It is comparable to looking at a photograph in a newspaper. We do not see the millions of dots that make up the image and the white spaces in between unless we look at it through a magnifying glass. Nevertheless, the dots are there. The same is true of moving images. Movie film is composed of hundreds of thousands of individual frames passing through a projector gate at the rate of 24 frames per second giving the illusion of continuous movement. We do not see the individual frames, only fluid action. Although our apparently solid, physical world is an illusion, it is a reality to us while we remain within our physical bodies, but there is another world of finer matter operating at a higher frequency in the spaces in between our own.

Quantum physicists now theorize that subatomic particles, known as 'dark matter', combine to produce the illusion of solidity in the same way that tones and overtones combine to create identifiable sounds. In a similar way, ghosts may be a transitory image indicative of a real presence, or a vibration in the ether created by residual personal energy but having no more physical substance than a sound wave created by a musical note. And like a note this residual energy will pass away echoing presumably into eternity but imperceptible to human beings. Consequently, we cannot afford to dismiss the existence of ghosts and other paranormal phenomena as unscientific and irrational simply because we are not aware of their presence. In fact, we can alter our perception to become aware of these other realities and we most often do so involuntarily when we are not so intensely focused on material matters.

OUR SIXTH SENSE

We have all experienced an involuntary shift in consciousness such as when we intuitively 'know' that someone will phone us moments before they do so, or when we meet someone who we had been thinking about the day before. Carl Jung, the Swiss analytical psychologist, whose own mystical experiences and insights formed the basis of today's modern psychotherapy, coined the useful term 'synchronicity' for these seeming coincidences.

So strong is our need to believe that our physical world is the only reality that more significant experiences such as the lucid dream in which we sense ourselves floating or flying are rarely accepted for what they are (genuine out-of-body experiences) and what they reveal about our true nature. However, we all possess an innate sixth sense which is merely an acute sensitivity to the more subtle forces and presences around us and not something abnormal or supernatural.

There are some people who are not only aware that they possess this heightened sensitivity but who have developed it to a remarkable degree. We call them psychics and attribute all manner of paranormal powers to them such as precognition (foreseeing future events), psychometry (picking up impressions from personal objects) and remote viewing (projecting consciousness to another location). Those psychics who claim to be able to communicate with the dead are known as mediums and are either regarded as gifted by those who have received comfort and closure from having been given compelling evidence of their loved ones' survival after death, or as charlatans by those who remain sceptical.

When the dead try to communicate with us we tend to block them out, either because we fear that acknowledging their presence will disturb our sense of reality or because we need to be grounded in the material world.

Many of us have been conditioned to dismiss their influence on our lives as coincidences or as figments of our imagination.

However, if we continue to ignore their presence they may intensify their efforts, moving small objects around and contriving to arrange uncanny coincidences. To this end, mediums are able to facilitate a meeting of minds between this world and the next, until we are willing and able to do this for ourselves.

There are those who are sceptical of mediums on principle and they accuse their 'gullible' clients of unconsciously colluding with the medium and of being highly selective in what they choose to remember from a session. Sceptics frequently charge psychics with 'fishing' for information, but they disregard the many thousands of mediums who offer personal information that the client could not possibly have known – consciously or otherwise. Although, no doubt, it does occur, many mediums do not tease clues from their clients or trick them into revealing information, then take credit for having 'channelled' those facts from the dead. In fact, they explicitly instruct their clients not to tell them anything until after the session has finished so that they will not be unduly influenced. Also, many refuse to accept money for themselves, agreeing only to accept a modest donation for their chosen charity.

CONVINCING EVIDENCE

Karin Page, founder of the Star of the East spiritual healing centre in Kent, England, had been seeing ghosts since the age of six, but it took a message from the 'other side' to finally convince her.

'One day my elderly mother-in-law promised me that she would come back after her death so that I would have proof of the survival of the soul. I didn't take it seriously at the time, but two months after her passing all the clocks in the house starting behaving strangely. They all showed a different time and a travelling alarm clock rolled off the shelf and crashed at my feet just as I was telling my daughter about how oddly they were all behaving. Another day the phone jumped off its holder on the wall and started swinging from side to side. Then the electric blanket and toaster switched themselves on. Each time I felt a chill in the air. It was Mary trying to tell me that she was with me.

The final proof came when I went to a spiritualist meeting and was told by a medium, who I'd never met before, that my husband's mother was trying to communicate, that her name was Mary and that she had died of cancer, both of which were true. She just wanted to say thank you for all the time I had looked after her. Then the medium said that Mary sent her love to my husband, my son and his girlfriend and she named them all which left me speechless. The only thing I couldn't understand was when she said, 'I'm with Emma now', because I didn't know of an Emma in the family. Mary had never mentioned her. Afterwards I learnt that Emma had been Mary's sister who had died 11 years earlier. Since then I have smelt Mary's talcum powder on many occasions and I know then that she is watching over me.'

POSITIVE BENEFITS

English medium Jill Nash believes that the job of a psychic

is to provide evidence of survival on the other side to give comfort to those left behind, not to impress clients with manifestations of ectoplasm and moving objects.

'Initially I talk to spirit in my mind and ask for their help. I feel their presence and can sense if they are male or female, but I never see them. I'm not communicating with the dead because nobody ever dies. They are the same personalities that they were in life. They are simply discarnate. I ask them to give me names and details that only the client will know which helps the client to relax and open up. Then I close my eyes and visualise drawing that person closer so that I am absorbed into their aura. When I make the connection I get excited. It's like having a present that you can't wait to open. At that point I usually feel a warmth and I might see a colour or a letter, or a combination of letters. If, for example I see them surrounded by blue I will know it is a communication issue and I'll ask them if they know of anyone whose name begins with the letter I've seen or a *place beginning with that letter that has a significance for them. That's the starting point. It's an entirely intuitive, automatic process. It's like picking at a strand in a ball of wool. It unravels slowly. When spirit has something to add it impresses itself in my mind. I only receive what spirit wants me to have at that time. It wouldn't help me or the client to know all the answers. We would stop working things out for ourselves and would only put an effort into something that would guarantee to reward our efforts.*

Unfortunately I couldn't tell my parents about my psychic experiences when I was young because they were very religious and were frightened of anything which challenged their faith. It made them uncomfortable. I used to sense a presence occasionally and my mother would shut me up by shouting, "I don't want to hear about dead people." But I was never scared because I know nothing really dies. Energy can't die. It can only be transformed.'

Jill sees a medium's role as helping the bereaved attain closure by facilitating a reunion with their loved ones.

'On one particularly memorable occasion I opened the door expecting to see a little elderly lady and instead saw her and her late husband. He walked in behind her. She was, of course, unaware that he was with her but I could see him plain as day, although he was fainter than a living person, almost transparent and there was nothing to see below the knee. He was tall and slim and when she sat down he stood behind her with a satisfied grin on his face as if he was thinking, 'At last, now I can tell her what I have been trying to say to her for months'.

As soon as we were settled he communicated to me telepathically, mind to mind, that he wanted me to tell her about a rose. Of course I didn't know what he meant, I hadn't met this lady before. But she did. He had apparently been trying to create a new type of rose by grafting and it hadn't taken while he was alive but he wanted her to keep the plant alive because he knew it was going to work. I *described the plant and the type of pot it was in and the fact that it was underneath the front window of their bungalow. Of course I had never seen their house but I could see it in my mind as he transferred his thoughts to mine.*

He wanted her to know that he was alright and that he was with her if she wanted to say anything or share her feelings. He told me to tell her that he often stood behind her when she sat in her armchair in the evenings and that if she felt something like a cobweb brushing against her cheek or a gentle pat on the head that it was only him reassuring her that he was still around. And as soon as I said that, she admitted that she had felt these things and had wondered if it was him, although she couldn't trust her own feelings or believe that he was really there.'

Jill's experiences have convinced her that the dead remain the same personalities they were on this side of life and recalls an incident with her father's ghost which revealed that he had not lost his mischievous sense of humour when he passed over.

'I went to an open day at Stanstead College which is popularly known as England's "psychic school". Some of the best mediums in the country were giving readings in various rooms and my friends and I began our "tour" in the main hall which was filled to capacity with several hundred people. We were standing at the back when the medium said that he had to interrupt his demonstration because he was being literally nagged by a spirit who was insisting he be allowed to come through. It was an elderly man by the name of Percy who had passed over 20 years ago. The medium described Percy and his habits including his compulsive need to pat his hair and the fact that one of his fingers was missing. And it was my dad! He had lost a finger in a factory accident when he was a young man. He just wanted to tell me that he was fine and that I had been right about what I told him would be waiting for him on the other side.

But the funniest thing was that when I went on to watch a demonstration of direct voice mediumship in the next room my dad's spirit followed me and said "hello" *again through that medium. The medium actually spoke in his voice which I recognised immediately. And if that wasn't enough he did it again in the next room through another medium, so then I had to tell him to stop and give someone else a turn!'*

BETTY SHINE

Some people are born with an acute psychic sensitivity or 'sixth sense' which enables them to see and communicate with discarnate spirits while others seem to develop this ability as the result of a traumatic event. Celebrity psychic Betty Shine, dubbed 'the World's number one healer' by the British popular press, was evidently blessed with more than her share of mediumistic gifts but was initially reluctant to develop them.

At the outbreak of the Second World War she was evacuated to the comparative safety of the English countryside with thousands of other children whose parents were desperate to save them from the dangers

The Fox family responding to mysterious rappings in their home at Hydesville, New York, as illustrated in literature of the time

:ances were the natural off-shoot of the rise of spiritualism, and were often taken part in by way of a diverting after-dinner game

'...[one of] many incidents where apparitions of the living appear in one location while their body resides elsewhere'

Sir Oliver Joseph Lodge (1851–1940) sought to bring together the transcendental world with the physical universe

of the London Blitz. One night a stray bomb landed near the house in which she was staying, blowing in all the windows and sending a large shard of glass into the headboard just an inch above her head. The shock appears to have stimulated her psychic sensitivity because the following night Betty began to see 'misty people' passing through her bedroom door, across the room and through the opposite wall. Even though they seemed oblivious to her she found their presence oddly reassuring and accepted her extraordinary psychic experiences as entirely natural. At the time she thought that everyone shared the same clairvoyant gifts until a friend assured her that seeing dead people was unusual to say the least.

While the traditional view is that ghosts are discarnate spirits haunting our world, Betty had a more rational interpretation for the visitations – she believed she was looking into another dimension in which the discarnate spirits were going about their normal activities. That would explain why many ghosts appear unaware of the living – they are not intruding into our world but we are peering into theirs.

At first Betty was reluctant to pursue her calling as a medium and healer, but by the time she had reached adulthood the build-up of suppressed psychic energy was making her physically ill. When she finally opened up to the power within she was overwhelmed by self-generated phenomena such as moving objects and disturbances which are commonly associated with poltergeist activity. 'I was seeing spirit faces everywhere – on the walls, in the carpet, everywhere and I would hear voices too as if I was suddenly able to hear people talking in the next room, only they weren't in this world but the next.'

She claims to have seen spirits in airports, on buses, in pubs and other public places, perhaps proving that our world and theirs are simply different facets of a greater, multi-dimensional reality and that there is no need to create a special atmosphere with candles and paranormal paraphernalia to communicate with our loved ones.

Most spirits are evidently content to co-exist with the living in a parallel plane, but according to Betty the dead can refuse to pass into their own world and instead linger in the presence of the living if they have 'unfinished business' to resolve.

On one occasion she sensed a dark entity over-shadowing a female patient and heard its voice in her own head saying; 'I will never leave her, she's mine.' As soon as she began praying for protection, Betty saw a bright white light appear around the entity putting it into silhouette. It was a man and as he was pulled away by some unseen force into the light he screamed. At the same moment, the woman instinctively covered her ears, though she later told Betty that she hadn't actually heard anything. After the session the woman told Betty that she had once been married to a possessive, sadistic man who had pursued her for years after she had left him before finally suffering a fatal heart attack on her doorstep. After his death she remarried but still felt his suffocating overbearing presence and had become chronically depressed. A few weeks after the exorcism the woman returned to Betty's healing centre radiant and relieved, finally free of the black cloud she felt had been smothering her for years.

Betty's experiences have given her a unique insight into the true nature of ghosts – or spirits as she prefers to call them. It is her understanding that we are not purely physical beings but possess an energy counterpart which animates the body and which can be seen by psychics as an aura of vital energy which radiates from each living person. It may be this residual energy which lingers in the atmosphere after death and is mistaken for a ghost while our spirit moves onto the next world.

THE PSYCHIC CLERIC

It is believed by some that everyone attends their own funeral in spirit, if only to see who has turned out to say goodbye. It is not uncommon for family members to see the deceased who often appear bemused at what they perceive as the fuss being made over their empty shell. Catholic sacristan Tina Hamilton often senses the presence of discarnate spirits during the funeral services at which she presides at St Thomas Church, Canterbury, England.

'I rarely see them, but I hear them and sense the force of their personality which has survived the death of the physical body. Sometimes I may even feel an arm around my shoulder. If it is a particularly strong presence they might try to communicate in which case I will hear them as another voice in my head. These are not my own thoughts. The tone of voice is quite distinct from my own. They tell me that they feel more alive than they did in life and will express frustration at not being able to be seen by their friends and family. Many express surprise at the number of people who have come to pay their respects while others seem amused at seeing a relative who didn't like them but who has reluctantly turned up out of a sense of duty. Curiously, it's usually their sense

of humour that touches me most strongly. I suspect it stems from the relief of having been unburdened of their earthly responsibilities and fears and the sense that they are now free from the constraints of the physical body.

I have been presiding over funeral services for more than 50 years and can truly say that I have never sensed a spirit that appeared disturbed, although I once conducted the funeral service for a teenage suicide who came through to say how sorry she was for having brought her parents so much pain. She asked me to tell them that it wasn't their fault. She had been suffering from depression and other problems which her family later confirmed to have contributed to her death.

Unfortunately being 'open' or receptive means that I attract lost souls like a moth to a flame. A psychic is like a lighthouse in a storm for those spirits who are disorientated after a fatal accident or sudden, unexpected death. Occasionally, when I am walking in the town I will hear someone calling my name and it is only when I turn round and find that there is no one *there that I'll realize that it is a spirit. So I'll ask who it is in my mind and what they want with me. If I have a name it helps me to establish an empathy and later I can find out who it was that I was helping. If they were unprepared for death they may be confused and even anxious as they can see us but most people can't see or hear them. So I tell them to remain calm and go into the light which is the threshold to the next dimension and moments later I will sense the presence fade and a feeling of peace or relief overwhelming me. A typical incident was that involving a young man who had just been killed on the dual carriageway while travelling down from Scotland. He couldn't understand how he could be in the town as he couldn't remember the end of the journey. He kept reliving the accident like a bad dream and couldn't accept that he had not survived the crash which had killed him. He identified himself by name so I was able to verify later. But even he wasn't distressed, simply confused. My experience leads me to believe that the soul does not suffer even a violent death, but is simply separated from the physical body by the event.'*

THE SOUL RESCUER

Exorcisms are rarely performed these days. The most common method of clearing a haunted house of earth-bound spirits today is a technique known as 'soul rescuing'.

British psychic Pamela Redwood typifies the new breed of 'sensitives' who can sense spirits – malign or otherwise – and work quietly to rid homeowners of their uninvited guests, bringing both parties peace of mind. She explains:

'What is sad is when someone cannot return to the light after their death because they are so attached to their life. I have cleared several houses where there have been disturbances or where the owner complains that they cannot live there because a certain room is cold even in the summer. They call me in and the first thing I pick up

on is a thickness in the atmosphere as if it is charged with an invisible presence. Sometimes my spirit guides will give me different colours and I will see that soul taken up through the ray of colour by my guides into the light and then the atmosphere will clear as if the room has been aired. I used to take the spirit up through my own body as I thought that I had to act as a channel for its return to the light but now the guides do it for me. Which is just as well as it could be very exhausting to be a host to someone else's spirit even for a few minutes. I would feel as if I'd absorbed their essence into my own being but occasionally if they were reluctant to go I would still have them with me when I went home. My daughter is very psychic and she would see me hobbling down the garden path, bent double like an old hag with a spirit on my shoulder and calmly say to her dad, "Mum's back and she's brought a ghost home."

I don't feel any fear when I do soul rescuing otherwise I couldn't do it. I know my guides are assisting me and it is work that needs to be done. Unfortunately people are *too eager to build anywhere these days and most of my work comes from people who have bought new houses built on the site of old burial grounds.*

You have to treat earth bound spirits as if they were still alive as they are the same personalities that they were in life. I once had to persuade the spirit of a pipe-smoking stubborn old man to pass over by promising him that he would have all the tobacco he could smoke if he went over to the other side!'

JOHN EDWARD

The young American medium John Edward (whose hugely popular TV show *Crossing Over* has been syndicated around the world) is one of a new generation of 'celebrity psychics'. His affability and commonsense approach have dispelled the suffocating gloom of Victorian spiritualism that gave mediumship a bad name with its candlelit séances, Ouija boards and obsession with ectoplasm. His extraordinary experiences demonstrate that spirits are not an unsettling paranormal phenomena but simply discarnate individuals who initiate contact with the living because they wish to assure their grieving loved ones that they are fine and to encourage them to move on with their own lives. John's experiences offer more insights into the true nature of the spirit world than were ever revealed by the mediums of the spiritualism movement. This suggests that we might now be ready to accept the existence of a wider reality. Perhaps we are even being prepared by being drip fed insights into the mysteries of the universe as an aid to our understanding, and evolution of our beliefs. John Edward was tested and his abilities verified under rigorous laboratory conditions by Gary Schwarz, professor of Psychology at the University of Arizona.

The first hint that he possessed an unusual talent came at an early age when he casually commented on events in his family history. These were events which he shouldn't have known about as they had occurred before he was born, yet he assured his parents that he remembered being there at the time. By the age of five he had informed his teachers that he could see a radiance around them. It was only much later that he learnt that not everyone could see these coloured auras. The first flowering of his psychic gifts began with visions of his maternal grandfather who had died in 1962, seven years before John was born. He saw the old man sitting at the dinner table next to his grandmother who took John's announcement that the old man was present as a comfort, even though she couldn't see her husband herself. John soon graduated to premonitions that relatives would drop by unexpectedly – a talent his mother soon learnt to take seriously and be grateful for.

John's particular ability for communicating with the departed developed in fits and starts during his adolescence. At first, the connection was tentative and difficult to decipher like receiving a weak signal from a distant radio station. There was considerable static obscuring the communications, but over time he learnt how to 'tune in' and filter out the interference. By the time he was 16, John was giving readings using tarot cards at psychic fairs, but then he began to receive messages for his clients in the form of intrusive thoughts which evidently did not originate in his own unconscious. To begin with they were simply names of dead people who were obviously attempting to communicate with his clients, but John felt uncomfortable being 'used' in this way. He resented the distraction as he was trying to concentrate on the cards. Predicting the future was fine as far as he was concerned, but talking to the dead spooked him. It also didn't sit well with his Catholic faith. Eventually, John began to trust these inner voices which became increasingly louder and more insistent. Subsequently, the names evolved into messages which he passed on to the delight of the living. The relief on the faces of anxious or grieving loved ones convinced him that what he was doing could not be a sin, but was instead a blessing.

Then one day, while he was still in his teens, he witnessed his first significant materialization. His aunt

Anna had teased him into reading the tarot cards which she regarded as little more than a child's magic trick. But when John looked up from the cards he saw a woman standing behind his aunt. She was a stout lady in her sixties, wearing a black dress and a flower-shaped brooch and she appeared to have only one leg.

John's description gave Aunt Anna a start. She immediately identified the mystery woman as her mother-in-law who had lost her leg through diabetes. Aunt Anna had never met her and neither had John because the old lady had died before he was born. But that was only the beginning. As John looked past his aunt, the old woman vanished and another figure appeared in her place. It was an impeccably dressed man in a pinstripe suit carrying a pocket watch. He was tall and slender with grey hair. This time Aunt Anna didn't recognize him from John's description so John opened up a dialogue with the man in his head. 'Show me something so that she will know who you are,' he said and was rewarded with a vision of the man lifting a large comb from his pocket and then pointing to a clock surrounded by flowers. The time on the clock read ten past two. The vision faded leaving John and his aunt none the wiser.

One week later, John's Uncle Carmine died unexpectedly of a heart attack. Only it wasn't such a shock to John because he had seen his uncle dying before his eyes in a particularly vivid vision three months earlier. It was so strong in fact that John had insisted that his uncle see a doctor, but the physicians gave the old man a clean bill of health.

Three months later at his uncle's wake, John stood before the coffin staring at a clock surrounded by roses. The time on the clock was ten minutes past two, the moment of his uncle's death.

It was a family tradition to mark the time of death in this way. That same day John learnt the identity of the man with the comb. A cousin recognized the description as that of Uncle Carmine's father who had been a barber. From that moment, John's psychic sensitivity went into overdrive.

INTERPRETING THE SPIRITS

The number of readings he was asked to give put enormous demands on his time, but the most taxing aspect was the sheer intellectual effort he had to make in order to interpret the subtle signs the spirits were showing him. Often they would use obscure references because they couldn't communicate directly, but on one occasion John learnt that there was a danger in trying too hard. During a reading for a recently bereaved lady, her dead husband kept showing John a bell. The reading had been going well up to that point and she had been able to verify everything John had passed on to her. But he was puzzled by the bell. He asked if she or her husband had had any connection with Philadelphia or Ben Franklin. Did they know of anyone called Ben or Franklin? It was only when John said that he kept seeing the image of a bell but couldn't think of another association for that image that the woman understood and became tearful. On the morning of his death her husband had given her a souvenir bell he had picked up on a business trip. 'If you ever need me, ring this and I'll be there,' he had said. Then he kissed his wife goodbye and went to work. He was killed in a car accident later that day. Sometimes a bell just means a bell.

As his fame spread, first by word of mouth and then through his TV show, John found his appointments diary filled to overflowing and the spirits crowding in, jostling for his attention in their eagerness to have their messages passed on to their loved ones. They would pull him to one side of the room and home him in on a particular member of the audience, then tease him with tantalizing clues. The atmosphere was good-natured, although often emotional, as friends and family members recognized a pet name or a half-forgotten incident which the spirit recalled to validate the evidence of their survival. Occasionally, the experience was dramatic. A victim of a car accident came through to give her version of events, offering unknown evidence implicating another vehicle's involvement which was subsequently verified by the police. And several murder victims described the guilty party which the family recognized as fitting the description of a suspect the police had had under observation but could not arrest for lack of evidence.

More often, though, spirits speak of mundane matters which sceptics argue is proof that mediumship is a dangerous delusion. If it was a genuine communication from the afterlife, they argue, then surely the spirit would have something profound to say about life after death. Instead, mediums usually report on routine family matters. John Edward contends that such minor personal details are more important for the grieving family as what they really need is proof that they are talking to their loved ones.

THE OUIJA BOARD

The Ouija (which is said to take its name from a combination of the French and German words for 'yes') was re-invented as a parlour game in 1898 at the height of the spiritualism craze by the Fuld brothers of Baltimore. It is the second highest-selling board game with 25 million sold in Europe and the USA to date and it continues to be available in toyshops and novelty stores around the world despite its dubious reputation.

The brothers may have been inspired by a similar technique used by the ancient Egyptians to contact their ancestors. The Egyptians used a ring suspended by a thread which they held over a board inscribed with mystic symbols. The inquirer then asked their questions and noted which symbols the ring indicated. The Ouija board works in a similar way. Participants place a finger on a pointer called a planchette (named after its creator) which moves on casters or felt with the slightest movement of the wrist, supposedly manipulated by the spirits, to spell out words using the alphabet printed on the board. Detractors argue that the 'spirit messages' originate in the participants' unconscious and that the imperceptible movements in the hand are caused by involuntary muscle contractions known as ideomotor actions. Whatever the source, there is no doubt that messages – many of them predicting death – have been recorded using this method.

Horror film fans will recall that it is through the use of the Ouija board that the little girl in *The Exorcist* becomes possessed, but in real life too there have been an alarming number of satanic-style murders and teenage suicides involving unstable and impressionable individuals who claim to have been acting on the instructions of demonic forces contacted through the board. It is marketed as a 'fun' game in which the 'players' consult the 'Mystifying Oracle', but the evidence suggests that in the wrong hands it can become dangerously addictive and can be profoundly disturbing to those who are psychologically unsound.

It is comparable to punching in a random phone number and hoping to connect with a family member, old friend or guru. Your call is far more likely to be picked up by a stranger who may find the temptation to tease or torment too good to resist. Even if the discarnate spirits who are attracted by this activity are not malevolent or intent on mischief, they may nevertheless influence how the players interpret their 'messages' simply by the fact that they are earthbound and therefore must be distressed or addictive personalities. This would account for the predominance of negative messages. Benign spirits are presumably beyond the influence of the board, enjoying their eternal rest.

The board itself may not be intrinsically bad, but it attracts the irresponsible and the immature who are not able to handle what they receive. If you have natural mediumistic ability, you won't need the board or any other focus object to induce the light trance state which will make you receptive to spirit communication.

However you view it, the Ouija board spells danger.

CHAPTER 5

The uninvited: possession

Not all cases of possession involve malevolent entities. Some appear to result from the awakening of dormant sub-personalities and even past life memories.

POSSESSION has decidedly negative connotations, but there have been incidents in which the uninvited spirit proved to have a benign purpose. In the summer of 1877, Mary Lurancy Vennum, a 13-year-old girl from Watseka, Illinois, suffered a series of convulsions, falling into a trance-like state for hours at a time. All efforts to awaken her failed.

THE VENNUM CASE

While she was in this state she spoke of seeing angels and a brother and sister who had died some years earlier. Shortly after this, Lurancy was subdued by a succession of dominant personalities who spoke through her, including a crotchety old woman called Katrina Hogan. The family resigned themselves to having their daughter committed to an asylum, but then a neighbouring family named Roff intervened. They persuaded Lurancy's parents to consult a doctor from Wisconsin who had treated their own daughter, also called Mary, in the months before her death. Mary Roff had suffered similar 'fits' in which she demonstrated clairvoyant abilities such as being able to read through a blindfold. These episodes had been witnessed by several eminent and respectable citizens of Watseka who were prepared to swear to what they had seen.

When Dr Stevens visited the Vennum house on 1 February 1878, Katrina Hogan was in control. At first she was cold and aloof, gazing abstractedly into space and ordering Dr Stevens to leave her be whenever he attempted to come near. But his persistence paid off and by and by Dr Stevens was able to draw out 'Katrina's' personal history. Soon another personality appeared, a young man named Willie Canning whose hold on Lurancy was erratic and offered little of value that the doctor could verify. With the parent's permission Dr

Stevens tried hypnosis and Lurancy reasserted herself but remained in a trance. She spoke of having been possessed of evil spirits, but that may have been her interpretation conditioned by her strict religious upbringing. Then events took an even more interesting turn.

Lurancy announced that she could see other spirits around her, one of whom was Mary Roff. Lurancy did not know Mary, who had died when Lurancy was just a year old, nor had she visited the Roff home.

Mrs Roff was present when her 'Mary' came through, speaking through Lurancy, but there is no suggestion that Lurancy was faking to impress or ingratiate herself with the dead girl's mother. The next morning 'Mary' calmly announced her intention to go 'home' by which she meant the Roff household. This naturally created some embarrassment for Mr and Mrs Vennum who were reluctant to have their daughter 'adopted' by a neighbour, but in her present state of mind it could have been argued that Lurancy was no longer their daughter. On 11 February, after much soul searching the Vennums agreed to let their daughter have her way.

En route they passed the Roff's old house where their daughter had died and 'Mary' insisted on being taken there, but she was eventually persuaded that it was no longer the family home. When she arrived at the new house she expressed delight at seeing her old piano and appeared to recognize the relatives who greeted her. Of course, none of this proves anything. Lurancy could have been shamming in order to secure attention. There was little risk in claiming to recognize the Roff's previous home as in those days everyone knew their neighbours and the history of the town. As for the piano, it was a fair assumption that it would have been in the family for some years and presumably had occupied pride of place in the previous house.

But even the most cynical witnesses were astonished to hear 'Mary' greet her old Sunday School teacher using her maiden name which Lurancy could not have known. Intrigued, the family subjected 'Mary' to a barrage of probing personal questions relating to seemingly insignificant incidents in her childhood which even the most imaginative impostor could not have faked. She satisfied them on all counts. She even remembered details of a family holiday and could name the spot where her pet dog had died. Most remarkably of all, she recalled the exact words written many years earlier by a medium during a séance who claimed to be channelling Mary's spirit communications.

Over the following weeks she recognized personal items that she had owned which Mr and Mrs Roff left unobtrusively in the hope of them being identified, but 'Mary' did more than acknowledge them. She would snatch them up in delight and offer some minor detail related to the item that her parents could verify. Clearly this was something more than a remarkable performance. It was a phenomenon, a rare example of benign possession which was similar in many ways to recorded cases of reincarnation, except that Mary Roff died when Lurancy was a small child. It could not be explained as a multiple personality disorder since 'Mary

Roff' evidently had intimate personal knowledge of the Roff family and her previous life.

On her arrival at the Roff house 'Mary' had predicted that she would be using Lurancy for three weeks after which she would return to the spirit world and allow Lurancy to continue with her life. She kept her word.

On the morning of 21 May, 'Mary Roff' vacated the body of her host and Lurancy returned to her parents. She later married and lived a normal happy life, but from time to time Mr and Mrs Roff would pay a visit at which time their daughter would make an appearance to reassure them that all was well. In gratitude for being allowed to say goodbye to her family, the benign spirit even intervened during the birth of Lurancy's first child, putting her into a trance to alleviate her pains.

SOUL MUSIC

Not all cases of possession are as inconvenient for their host as the Mary Lurancy Vennum case, or as unpleasant as that portrayed in *The Exorcist*. The following is a case in point.

On New Year's Day 1970, the musicologist Sir Donald Tovey gave his expert opinion on the authenticity of certain compositions by Beethoven and Liszt which had reputedly been 'channelled' through London medium Mrs Rosemary Brown. He then took the opportunity to share his insights into why the world was now ready to receive these gifts from heaven.

'To understand himself fully [Man] should become aware of the fact that he does not consist merely of a temporary form which is doomed to age and die. He has an immortal soul which is housed in an immortal body and endowed with a mind that is independent of a physical brain. In communication through music and conversation, an organized group of musicians who have departed from your world are attempting to establish a precept for humanity; i.e. that physical death is a transition from one state of consciousness to another

wherein one retains one's individuality. The realization
of this fact should assist man to a greater insight into his
own nature and potential super-terrestrial activities.'

This was profound and revealing stuff. The only problem was that Sir Donald Tovey had been dead for some years when he gave this 'lecture' through the auspices of Mrs Brown. Sceptics might say that it was extremely convenient that Mrs Brown was able to channel both the great composers and a respected music critic to verify their work, but there was no disputing the fact that the music was of a very high quality and that its complexity was way beyond Mrs Brown's humble talents. By all accounts she was a pianist of moderate ability and her knowledge of music was rudimentary at best. Yet for the last five years she had been taking dictation from Liszt, Beethoven, Chopin, Schubert, Brahms and Debussy at a speed she could barely keep up with and, according to a number of influential musicologists, in their distinctive style.

There was one problem, however, and this appears to be the key to the whole mystery. The music was 'first class' according to one critic, but it was not music of genius. If the great composers were active again on the other side, why then did they not produce masterworks rather than highly proficient imitations which any serious music student could conceivably have created to impress their professor? And why choose Mrs Brown? Admittedly she was a practising medium, but surely they would have attempted to commune with a serious musician who would have done their new compositions justice and with whom they would have had a greater empathy.

Although this appears to be a clear case of possession, there is a distinct possibility that it might be an example of split personality disorder, albeit a highly productive one. Word association tests carried out by researcher Whately Carrington in 1935 with the mediums Osborne Leonard and Eileen Garrett suggest that the 'controls' which mediums claim are the mediators between themselves and the spirits might actually be their own sub-personalities and that these sink back into the unconscious when the dominant personality reclaims control (when the medium wakes from their trance). In comparing their responses to key words Carrington discovered that the controls were mirror images of the mediums – a characteristic of multiple personalities. This would account for the mediums' inability to remember what they had channelled and also for the mysterious appearance of their phenomenal latent talents. At the same time it might also explain why the music was technically impressive, but not of the quality that such men of genius would be expected to produce if they had been given a chance to continue working from the 'other side'.

This theory does not explain incidents of genuine mediumship in which the medium has communicated personal information that he or she could not have had access to, unconsciously or otherwise, and which was subsequently verified as correct by the bereaved. But it could be significant that subjects have exhibited telepathic abilities under hypnosis, such as sharing physical sensations with the hypnotist, which might suggest that when the left side of the brain (the objective or ordinary mind) is put to sleep, the right side of the brain (also known as the subjective or subliminal mind) might then be receptive to spirit communications.

THE ARTIST WITHIN

Automatic art, or automatism to give it its clinical name, is not a recent phenomenon. In the 1930s, the American psychiatrist Dr Anita Muhl experimented with the technique to see if she could connect with her mentally ill patients. Against all the laws of logic and the expectations of her medical colleagues, many of

Dr Muhl's patients produced impressive prose, paintings, sketches and musical compositions with their passive hand (the one they did not normally use to write with), with both hands simultaneously, occasionally writing and drawing upside down or even backwards. A number of patients were even able to draw 'blind', without looking at the paper. All of this was done fluidly, at great speed and without error. Dr Muhl believed that these latent talents originated in the unconscious, but there are those on the fringes of the scientific community who suspect that there might be spirits or a past-life personality at work. What other explanation, they say, can account for the feats of former antiques dealer John Tuckey who can complete epic Dickensian novels in a distinctive nineteenth-century copperplate script in a matter of weeks? Or what about the remarkable achievements of the Brazilian automatic artist Luiz Gasparetto who can produce two paintings in the style of different great masters simultaneously, one working upright and the other created upside down. Often Gasparetto will take less than a minute to produce a sketch worthy of Cézanne or Manet – and he doesn't even use brushes. He will employ his fingers and even his toes to create a one-minute masterpiece.

There is another theory to account for such

accomplishments and this is that each of us contains more than one personality which are normally controlled by the dominant persona that has, effectively, taken the driving seat.

THE THREE CLARAS

When psychiatrist Morton Prince placed patient Clara Fowler under hypnosis he unwittingly freed two contrasting personalities, each unaware of the other. Clara had been morose, subdued and suffered from depression while her two alter egos could not have been more different. One was considerably more mature and self-assured while the second, which identified herself as 'Sally', was a lively and mischievous little girl who would 'possess' Clara at inconvenient moments. Without warning 'Sally' would take over for hours at a time and when Clara regained control she would find herself in another part of town, bewildered as to how she got there. At the height of her influence, 'Sally' moved to another town, secured a job as a waitress for two weeks and then vacated her host who consequently had to talk her way out of a job she hadn't applied for and find her own way back home.

Spiritualists might interpret these experiences as evidence of possession, while a psychiatrist would regard them as sub-personalities, but if they are merely aspects of our unconscious why then do they create a separate personal history for themselves, speak in another voice and exhibit talents which the dominant personality does not possess? Could it be that they are, in fact, transitory memories and talents from that person's former lives which have been reawakened?

THE QUESTION OF REINCARNATION

A belief in ghosts does not necessarily lead to an acceptance of reincarnation – the idea that we all experience a series of lives in order to achieve enlightenment or self-realization – but the cyclic nature of life as reflected in the changing seasons and the principle of evolution suggests that it is not only logical but highly desirable that we need more than one life in order to fulfil our full potential. While the evidence for reincarnation may be seen to be as compelling as that for the existence of spirits, it was not until the late 1960s when the Beatles popularly introduced the West to meditation and mind-expanding drugs that this spiritual world view entered Western consciousness, although it had been a core belief of the Celts and the Ancient Greeks.

In post-war Britain the concept of reincarnation was considered to be an alien idea peculiar to the exotic Eastern philosophies of Hinduism, Shintoism and Buddhism. So when, in 1962, a Catholic father announced that his daughters were living proof of the existence of reincarnation it was seen as a challenge to the authority of the Church which had declared the concept heretical.

John Pollock had lost his first two daughters, Joanna,

11, and Jacqueline, 6, in May 1957 when a driver lost control of her car and careered into the children near their home in Hexham, Northumberland. Pollock assumed that God had taken his girls to punish him for believing in reincarnation, but a year later, when his wife learnt that she was pregnant, Pollock became convinced that the souls of the two girls would be reborn in order to demonstrate that the church was wrong to deny the natural process of death and rebirth. When his wife's gynaecologist informed the couple that they were to expect a single child Pollock assured him he was wrong – there would be twins, both girls. On 4 October 1958, he was proved correct.

The twins were monozygotic (meaning they developed from a single egg) yet the second twin Jennifer, was born with a thin white line on her forehead in the same place that her dead sister Jacqueline had sustained a wound while falling from her bicycle. Her parents were also puzzled by the appearance of a distinctive birth mark on her left hip, identical to the one that Jacqueline had.

The girls grew up in Whitley Bay, but when they were three and a half their father took them back to Hexham and was astonished to hear the girls point out places they had never seen in this life and talk about where they had played, even though they had left the town before they could walk. They knew when they were approaching their school although it was out of sight, and they recognized their old home as they passed it although their father had said nothing.

Six months later, they were given Joanna and Jacqueline's toy box. They identified all their dead sisters' dolls by name. They were also observed playing a game that their mother, Florence Pollock, found disturbing. Jennifer lay on the floor with her head in Gillian's lap, play-acting that she was dying and her sister would say, 'The blood's coming out of your eyes. That's where the car hit you.' Neither parent had discussed the accident with the children. On another occasion their mother heard them screaming in the street. When she came out she saw them clutching each other and looking terrified in the direction of a stationary car with its motor running. The girls were crying, 'The car! It's coming at us!'

The possibility that they might be the reincarnation of their elder, deceased sisters brought no comfort to their mother who could not reconcile the evidence of her own eyes with the Church's edict that belief in reincarnation was a mortal sin. For this reason she made an excellent impartial witness. To Florence Pollock's relief, however, the incident with the car marked the end of the affair. At the age of five the girls abruptly ceased to seem conscious of the connection with their former lives and developed into normal, healthy children.

This is consistent with a belief that at the age of five all children lose their link with the other world. At this point, to borrow an expression from the esoteric tradition, 'the veil comes down'. Children cease to play with imaginary friends and become grounded in the 'real' world. And perhaps something of the magic of childhood and worldly innocence dies with it.

CHAPTER 6

Haunted houses

Ghosts do not only haunt crumbling castles, but have been sighted in the homes of celebrities, hotels, aircraft, restaurants and even a Toys "R" Us store.

If any site deserves its formidable reputation for spectral sightings it is the Tower of London whose weathered stones are soaked in the blood of countless executed martyrs and traitors. It is said that the walls still echo with the screams of those who were tortured there during the most violent chapters of English history and with the muffled sobbing of those innocents who were put to death for displeasing the monarchy. It is a place of pain where the unquiet souls of those who were imprisoned relive their suffering seemingly for eternity with no prospect of finding peace.

THE BLOODY TOWER

Its long and bloody history began almost 1,000 years ago in 1078 when William the Conqueror built the White

Tower in a strategically significant location on the River Thames. Over the next 500 years, the 18-acre site was developed into a formidable fortress within which a succession of kings exercised their divine right over the lives and deaths of their subjects; former friends, wives and enemies alike.

By the dawn of the seventeenth century, English royalty had moved to more palatial quarters and the Tower became a soldier's garrison and prison. On the morning of their execution, condemned prisoners were ceremoniously paraded past jeering crowds to the scaffold erected on nearby Tower Hill where they would be beheaded, or hung, drawn and quartered, and then their bodies would be brought back for burial within the walls of the Tower. These processions of sombre figures have been seen in modern times by sentries who were able to describe accurately the uniforms worn by the burial party.

Among the Tower's most illustrious residents were the young princes Edward and Richard who were declared illegitimate and imprisoned in the so-called Bloody Tower by their ambitious uncle the Duke of Gloucester. It is believed by some that he ordered their murder so that he could be crowned King Richard III. The princes have been sighted several times walking hand in hand through the chilly corridors after dusk, possibly in search of their murderous uncle. Their alleged murderer has not been seen skulking around the scene of his hideous crimes which may suggest that his conscience was clear. Given the murdered princes' sense of injustice or revenge, ghosts appear to be an emotional residue rather than a conscious presence.

This is borne out by the nature of the other ghosts which haunt the Tower – they are all victims, not the perpetrators, of the many crimes which took place there. Edward IV, father to the murdered princes, ordered the death of his Lancastrian rival Henry VI on 21 May 1471 at the end of the War of the Roses, but it is not Edward who haunts the oratory in the Wakefield Tower where the killing took place, but Henry who has been seen seated outside the oratory praying that his soul might find peace.

The second wife of Henry VIII is said to still walk in the Tower Chapel where she made her peace with her God before she was despatched to his heavenly kingdom in 1536. She is reported to have been seen leading a spectral procession through the chapel both with and without her head.

One of the most gruesome episodes in the Tower's history was the botched execution of Margaret Pole, Countess of Salisbury. Margaret was 70 years old when she was condemned to death in 1541 by Henry VIII, even though she posed no threat to his dynasty. Standing resolutely regal on the scaffold, she refused to submit to the hooded executioner who waited for her to rest her head on the block, but instead she commanded him to sever her head from her neck where she stood. When he refused she fled, forcing him to pursue her around Tower Green swinging the axe like a serial killer in a modern splatter movie. Within minutes the hideous spectacle was at an end; the last female Plantagenet had been hacked to pieces. If you find that too gruesome to be true, you only have to ask permission to remain in the Tower after dark on 27 May, the anniversary of her execution, to see the scene re-enacted by the principal players themselves as Margaret's ghost tries once again to outrun her executioner.

Other apparitions are less active. The headless ghost of James Crofts Scott, the illegitimate son of King Charles II, for example, is said to do little more than walk the battlements connecting the Bell and Beauchamp Towers dressed in cavalier attire. Apparently, James was not satisfied with being made Duke of Monmouth as compensation for losing the crown to his uncle, James II, in 1685, and chose to assert his claim by force of arms. His rebellion was short lived and he paid for his disloyalty by forfeiting his head.

Arguably the most tragic figure to haunt the site of her untimely death is Lady Jane Grey who was a pawn in the Duke of Northumberland's stratagem to usurp the English crown from the rightful heir, Mary Tudor. Lady Jane, who was only 15, ruled for less than two weeks before she was arrested and condemned to death together with her young husband and his father in February 1554. Her grieving ghost has been sighted by reliable witnesses on several occasions. In 1957, two sentries swore they witnessed the apparition of the young queen form from a ball of light on the roof of the Salt Tower while others have reported seeing the spirit of the Duke sobbing at the window of the Beauchamp Tower as he had done on the morning of his execution.

One would imagine that a spell in the Tower would be sufficient to bring even the most rebellious subjects to their senses, but Sir Walter Raleigh incurred the monarch's displeasure more than once. In 1592, Queen Elizabeth I ordered him to be thrown into the Tower, but upon his release he continued to bait the Queen in the belief that he was too popular to be executed. After Elizabeth's death, James I lost patience with Raleigh's preening and boasting and had him convicted on a trumped up charge of treason. He was eventually freed in 1616 on condition that he journeyed to the New World in search of gold to fill the royal coffers, but he ignored the King's express orders not to plunder from England's Spanish allies and was beheaded on his return. His ghost still walks the battlements near what were once his apartments in the Bloody Tower.

Not all of the Tower's non-corporeal residents have returned because they cannot rest or because they desire revenge. The ghost of Henry Percy, 9th Earl of Northumberland, has been sighted strolling amiably on the roof of the Martin Tower where he enjoyed walks during his enforced incarceration which began in 1605. Percy, who had been implicated in the Gunpowder Plot, was one of the few prisoners to have been allowed to keep his head and he whiled away the days debating the latest advances in science and other subjects with other educated nobles until his release 16 years later. Percy owed his release to his willingness to pay a fine of

£30,000. Since he is clearly reluctant to leave the Tower centuries after his death, perhaps he feels he hasn't had his money's worth.

THE GHOSTS OF GLAMIS

If the typical collection of 'true' ghost stories is to be believed, every castle in the British Isles has its own resident ghost. Whether there is any truth in that or not, Glamis Castle in Scotland certainly has more than its share.

Glamis is the oldest inhabited castle north of the border and is renowned for being both the setting for the tragedy of Macbeth and also the ancestral home of the late Queen Mother, Elizabeth Bowes-Lyon. It also has an unenviable reputation as the most haunted castle in the world. Not all the ghosts are tortured souls. In the Queen Mother's sitting room the ghost of a cheeky negro servant boy has been sighted playing hide and seek. There is no doubt that the legends of Glamis provide more gruesome thrills than an old-fashioned Gothic thriller. However, fact and fiction are so creatively intertwined that it is now impossible to know which is which.

Several visitors and guests have been distressed by the apparition of a pale and frightened young girl who has been seen pleading in mute terror at a barred window. Legend has it that she was imprisoned after having had her tongue cut out to keep her from betraying a family secret – but what that secret might be remains a mystery. In the 1920s, a workman was said to have accidentally uncovered a hidden passage and to have been driven to the edge of insanity by what he found there. Allegedly, the family bought his silence by paying for his passage to another country. There are also tales of a hideously deformed heir who was locked in the attic and an ancient family curse of which the 15th Earl is reputed to have said: 'If you could only guess the nature of the secret, you would go down on your knees and thank God that it was not yours.'

The family's troubles are believed to date from 1537 when the widow of the 6th Lord Glamis was accused of witchcraft and burned at the stake. From that day to this her ghost has been seen on the anniversary of her death on the roof of the clock tower, bathed in a smouldering red glow. Several of the castle's 90 rooms have a dark and bloody history. King Malcolm II of Scotland was murdered in one of them and the floor was boarded because the bloodstains could not be scrubbed clean. It is thought that this may have been the inspiration for the murder of King Duncan, Thane of Glamis, in Shakespeare's play *Macbeth*.

During the years of inter-clan warfare, the castle acquired an entire chamber of vengeful spirits when men from the Ogilvy clan were given refuge from their enemies in the dungeon, but were then betrayed by their host who walled them up alive. When the wall was torn down a century later, it is said that their skeletons were found in positions which suggested that they had been gnawing on their own flesh. The Scottish novelist Sir

Walter Scott, who considered himself a hardy adventurer, braved a night there in 1793 and lived to regret it: 'I must own, that when I heard door after door shut, after my conductor had retired, I began to consider myself as too far from the living, and somewhat too near the dead.'

In his classic survey of supernatural stories, *The Ghost Book* (1936), Lord Halifax recounts the unnerving experience of a Mrs Monro who was the guest of the new owners Lord and Lady Strathmore in November 1869, a story later verified by Lady Strathmore herself.

'In the middle of the night, Mrs Monro awoke with a sensation as though someone was bending over her; indeed, I have heard that she felt a beard brush her face. The night-light having gone out, she called her husband to get up and find the matches. In the pale glimmer of the winter moon she saw a figure pass into the dressing room. Creeping to the end of the bed she felt for and found the matchbox and struck a light, calling out loudly, "Cam, Cam, I've found the matches."

To her surprise she saw that he had not moved from

her side. Very sleepily he grumbled, "What are you bothering about?"

At that moment they heard a shriek of terror from the child in the dressing room. Rushing in, they found him in great alarm, declaring that he had seen a giant. They took him into their own room, and while they were quieting him off to sleep they heard a fearful crash as if a heavy piece of furniture had fallen.

At that moment the big clock had struck four.

Nothing more happened, and the next morning Mr Monro extracted a reluctant promise from his wife to say nothing about her fright, as the subject was known to be distasteful to their host. However, when breakfast was half over, [another guest] Fanny Trevanion, came down, yawning and rubbing her eyes and complaining of a disturbed night. She always slept with a night-light and had her little dog with her on her bed. The dog, she said, had awakened her by howling. The night-light had gone out, and while she and her husband were hunting for matches they heard a tremendous crash, followed by the clock striking four. They were so frightened they could not sleep again.

Of course, this was too much for Mrs Monro, who burst out with her story. No explanation was offered and the three couples agreed on the following night to watch in their respective rooms. Nothing was seen, but they all heard the same loud crash and rushed out onto the landing. As they stood there with scared faces the clock again struck four. That was all; and the noise was not heard again.'

PURSUED BY DREAMS

So far this follows the customary ghost story tradition, but then it becomes even more intriguing. On the night of 28 September, Lord Halifax was staying at Tullyallan Castle, a modern comfortable home with no hint of a ghost when he dreamt that he was back at Glamis, which had once been his late brother-in-law's home. It was a fearful dream in which he was pursued by a huge man with a long beard. In a desperate effort to keep the ghost at bay – for in his dream Lord Halifax knew the man was dead – he offered him broken chains which a maid had found hidden in the hollow space below the grate in his room. His story continues:

> '"You have lifted a great weight off me," sighed the ghost.
> "Those irons have been weighing me down ever since ..."
> "Ever since when?" asked his Lordship.
> "Ever since 1486," replied the ghost.'

The next moment Halifax awoke.

In itself the dream would not be significant, but on the very same night the daughter of Lord Castletown was staying at Glamis unaware of the ghosts who were said to haunt several of its rooms. According to Lord Halifax:

> 'During the night she awoke with the feeling that someone was in the room and sitting up in bed she saw, seated

in front of the fire, a huge old man with a long flowing beard. He turned his head and gazed fixedly at her and then she saw that although his beard rose and fell as he breathed the face was that of a dead man . . . after a few minutes he faded away and she went to sleep again.'

Years later, Lord Halifax had the chance to relate his dream to Lady Strathmore who remarked on the uncanny 'coincidence' and she gave a start when he mentioned the year of the ghost's death. Apparently Glamis' most infamous ghost, Earl Beardie, was murdered in 1486.

THIRTEEN GUESTS

The Winchester Mansion in San Jose, California is unique among haunted houses. It was built by ghosts. Haunted houses are usually host to the restless spirits of their previous occupants, but in the case of the Winchester Mystery House, as it is known locally, its ghosts were not only invited to make themselves at home, they even directed the owner as to how they wanted the house built.

In 1884, Mrs Winchester was grieving for the loss of both her son and her husband who had made his fortune manufacturing the famous Winchester repeating rifle – 'The gun that won the West'. In her grief Mrs Winchester became convinced that the restless spirits of those killed by her husband's weapons would torment her unless she devoted the rest of her life to extending the mansion according to their wishes so that they could while away eternity in comfort.

Every evening she presided over a spooky supper at a long dining table laid for 13, herself and 12 invisible guests. The servants indulged her eccentricities as they were allowed to partake of the leftovers. After dinner the widow conducted a private séance to hear the spirits' latest plans which she would interpret for the workmen the next morning. Either the spirits had a sense of mischievous humour or else Mrs Winchester may have been deliberately trying to disorientate her guests. The house features a number of staircases leading up to the ceiling and doors which open onto a brick wall or a sheer drop. In one particular room there is a single entrance but three exits on the facing wall, one of which leads to an 8 ft drop into the kitchen on the floor below and another into a windowless room. The door to this room has no handle on the other side, perhaps to entrap a curious ghost or because Mrs Winchester believed it wouldn't need a door knob as a ghost could supposedly float through the door!

The ghosts seem to have had an obsession with the number 13. They demanded that every new staircase should have 13 steps and new rooms must have 13 windows. The chandeliers should boast 13 bulbs and the same number of coat hooks should be available in case they needed to hang up their spectral raincoats. There were even 13 fan lights in the greenhouse in case the spirits fancied a spell of hot house horticulture.

By the time Mrs Winchester passed away on 5 September 1922 at the age of 82, she had devoted the last 38 years of her life to extending the mansion which by then had grown to 160 rooms.

In the 1990s, a pair of paranormal investigators stayed overnight in the house and were aroused by music from a ghostly organ which, on examination, proved to be disconnected. Moments later they were unnerved by a violent disturbance as the house was shaken to its foundations. In the morning they asked the tour guides if any damage had been caused by the earthquake and were dumbfounded to learn that no tremors had been reported in the area, although in 1906 the destructive San Francisco earthquake had struck at the very same time and severely damaged part of the house.

Not surprisingly, perhaps, the mansion has become a popular tourist attraction, and in case any visitor sneers at the idea of a house being built for ghosts the guides are ready to assure them that at least three spirits walk the house – a young female servant, a carpenter who had died at the site and the indomitable Mrs Winchester, whom staff have seen in Victorian dress, sitting at a table. When they asked their colleagues why they needed someone dressed up as Mrs Winchester they were told that no one was employed to dress up and play the part.

BORLEY RECTORY

During the 1930s and 1940s, Borley Rectory acquired a sinister reputation as 'The Most Haunted House in England'. This unimposing vicarage near Sudbury, Essex, was built in 1863 on the site of a Benedictine monastery which had a dark and unholy history. It was said that a Borley monk had seduced a local nun and the pair had planned to elope. They were caught and the monk was executed and the nun was walled up alive in the cellar.

The first incumbent of the new rectory was the Reverend Bull who built a summerhouse overlooking a path known as the Nun's Walk. From there he sometimes observed the materializations of the weeping woman as she wandered the gardens searching for her murdered lover. Bull often invited guests to join him on his ghost watch but few stayed long enough to share his vigil. Once they had caught the nun peering in through their ground floor bedroom window they made their excuses and cut their visit short. Bull's four daughters and his son Harry resigned themselves to regular sightings of the forlorn spirit drifting across the lawn in broad daylight, but when it was joined by a spectral coach and horses galloping up the drive, the surviving Bull children decided to move on. Their father had died in the Blue Room in 1892 and his son Harry in the same room in 1927.

At the end of the 1920s, the Reverend Eric Smith and his wife took up residence, shrugging off stories of phantom carriages and sobbing nuns.

They had barely had time to unpack their belongings before a burst of poltergeist activity encouraged them to sell up and move out. However, during their two-year tenure they took the unusual step of calling in the man who was to ensure Borley a place in paranormal history – ghost hunter extraordinaire Harry Price.

Price was a notorious self-publicist and one-time music hall conjurer who had hoped to make a name for himself by exposing fake mediums and debunking the whole spiritualist movement as mere charlatanism. The more he saw at first hand, however, the more convinced he became that some of it was genuine. Eventually, he came to the conclusion that he was more likely to fulfil his ambition of getting into Debrett's (a directory of the rich and famous) if he could find proof of life after death than if he merely unmasked a few fraudulent mediums.

At the invitation of the Reverend Smith, and later with the encouragement of the next tenants Mr and Mrs Foyster, Price recorded incidents involving phantom footsteps, flying objects and even physical attacks: on one notable occasion Mrs Foyster was even turned out of bed by an invisible assailant. She was also the subject of unintelligible messages scrawled on the walls. Her husband had the house exorcized but the spirits persisted. The servants' bells rang of their own accord and music could be heard coming from the chapel even though no one was in the building. The Foysters admitted defeat and left the spooks in peace. Subsequent owners fared little better. Eventually, the house burned down in a mysterious fire in 1939 as predicted by a spirit 11 months earlier during a séance conducted on the site by Price. Witnesses stated that they saw phantoms moving among the flames and the face of a nun staring from a window.

THE GHOST-HUNTER'S BOOK

Price published his findings in 1940 under the title *The Most Haunted House in England*, boasting that it presented 'the best authenticated case of haunting in the annals of psychical research'. The book was an instant bestseller providing as it did some escapism in the first anxious months of the Second World War and quickly established a non-fiction genre of its own – the haunted house mystery. Its success generated a slew of similar books by self-proclaimed experts and sufficient interest in Price to spawn several (highly critical) biographies. Price revelled in his new found fame, but it was short-lived. He died in 1948 having spent the last 40 years of his life providing what he believed to be irrefutable evidence of the paranormal. But he was not allowed to rest in peace. In the decade after his death there were spiteful personal attacks on his reputation by rival ghost hunters alleging that Price had faked certain phenomena. Mrs Smith wrote to the *Church Times* denying that she and her husband had claimed that the rectory was haunted, although it is thought that she may have done this to ingratiate herself with the Church authorities who had been embarrassed by the whole affair. An investigation by the SPR, conducted by members who were openly hostile to Harry Price, concluded that he had manipulated certain facts to substantiate his claims and that other incidents probably had a 'natural explanation'. Price's reputation was seriously undermined, but the fact remains that the Reverend Bull and his family had said that they had seen spirits before Price arrived on the scene. (Miss Ethel Bull had reported seeing a phantom figure at the end of her bed and of sensing another sitting on the end of the bed on more than one occasion.) Also Mrs Foyster appears to have provoked an outbreak of genuine poltergeist activity. Price himself suspected that she augmented it with some phenomena of her own creation, perhaps because she craved attention, or at least so as not to disappoint his expectations.

Either way, questions remain. If Price had faked phenomena, why did he rent the rectory for a year after Mrs Foyster moved out, only to admit that there was nothing anomalous to report? He would have had more than enough time and opportunity to stage something truly astounding to substantiate his claims. The inactivity during that period suggests that the spirits might have been attracted by the presence of the Reverend Bull and Mrs Foyster who perhaps possessed mediumistic abilities.

A subsequent investigation by the SPR under R.J.

Hastings unearthed previously unpublished letters from the Reverend Smith and his wife to Price, written in 1929, in which Smith states emphatically that 'Borley is undoubtedly haunted'. This discovery forced the SPR to revise its earlier findings. Price had been vindicated. Whatever short cuts Price may have taken to enhance his reputation as Britain's foremost ghost hunter it cannot be denied that there was something out of the ordinary occurring at Borley.

A footnote to the Borley investigation was added in the 1950s by the novelist Dennis Wheatley, author of *The Devil Rides Out* and dozens of occult thrillers:

'Kenneth Allsop, the book reviewer of the Daily Mail, *told me that when Borley was in the news he was sent down to do an article on it, and with him he took a photographer. Borley was then being 'debunked' so that had to be the tone of the article. But when the photographer developed his photos the figure of a nun could be quite clearly seen on one of them. He took it to*

Allsop, who took it to his editor, but the editor said, "No,
I just daren't print it."'

A curious postscript to the Borley saga occurred on 28
August 1977 when ley line expert Stephen Jenkins visited
the area with a view to seeing if there was anything to
the theory that the 'curious manifestations' might be
linked to a spider's web of ley line alignments.

'*The time was precisely 12.52 pm and we were driving*
south-west along the minor road which marks the north
end of the hall ground, when on the road in front in the
act of turning left into a hedge (I mean our left across the
path of the car), instantaneously appeared four men in
black – I thought them hooded and cloaked – carrying a
black, old fashioned coffin, ornately trimmed with silver.
The impression made on both of us was one of absolute
physical presence, of complete material reality. Thelma and
I at once agreed to make separate notes without comparing
impressions. We did so and the descriptions tallied exactly,

except that she noted the near left bearer turned his face towards her. I did not see this as I was abruptly braking at the time. What I had seen as a hood, she described as a soft tall hat with a kind of scarf falling to the left shoulder, thrown across the cloak body to the right. The face was that of a skull.

'The next day we returned to the spot at precisely the same time and took a picture. It is a Kodak colour slide. In the hedge near the gap where the 'funeral party' vanished (there's a path there leading to Belchamp Walter churchyard) is a short figure apparently cloaked, his face lowered with a skull-like dome to the head . . . I hazard a guess that the dress of the coffin bearer is that of the late 14th century. There seems to be no local legend of a phantom funeral.'

WEIRD NIGHT IN A HAUNTED HOUSE

While Harry Price was accused of having falsified some of the 'evidence' and having made fraudulent claims in order to boost his reputation as Britain's foremost ghost hunter, the following article from the *Daily Mirror* of 14 June 1929 suggests that Harry's first visit to Borley was lively enough without the need for artificial aids or exaggeration:

'Weird Night In "Haunted" House'

from our Special Correspondent

There can no longer be any doubt that Borley Rectory, near here, is the scene of some remarkable incidents. Last night Mr Harry Price, Director of the National Laboratory For Psychical Research, his secretary Miss Lucy Kaye, the Reverend G.F. Smith, Rector of Borley, Mrs Smith and myself were witnesses to a series of remarkable happenings. All these things occurred without the assistance of a medium or any kind of apparatus. And Mr Price, who is a research expert only and not a spiritualist, expressed himself puzzled and astonished at the results. To give the phenomena a thorough test however, he is arranging for a séance to be held in the rectory with the aid of a prominent London medium.

The first remarkable happening was the dark figure that I saw in the garden. We were standing in the Summer House at dusk watching the lawn when I saw the 'apparition' which so many claim to have seen, but owing to the deep shadows it was impossible for one to discern any definite shape or attire. But something certainly moved along the path on the other side of the lawn and although I quickly ran across to investigate it had vanished when I reached the spot.

Then as we strolled towards the rectory discussing the figure there came a terrific crash and a pane of glass from the roof of a porch hurtled to the ground. We ran inside and upstairs to inspect the room immediately over the porch but found nobody. A few seconds later we were descending the stairs, Miss Kaye leading, and Mr Price behind me when something flew past my head, hit an iron stove in the hall and shattered. With our flash lamps we inspected the broken pieces and found them to be sections of a red vase which, with its companion, had been standing on the mantelpiece of what is known as the Blue Room which we had just searched. Mr Price was the only person behind me and he could not have thrown the vase at such an angle as to pass my head and hit the stove below.

We sat on the stairs in darkness for a few minutes and just as I turned to Mr Price to ask him whether we had waited long enough something hit my hand. This turned out to be a common moth ball and had apparently dropped from the same place as the vase. I laughed at the idea of a spirit throwing moth balls about, but Mr Price said that such methods of attracting attention were not unfamiliar to investigators.

Finally came the most astonishing event of the night. From one o'clock till nearly four this morning all of us, including the rector and his wife, actually questioned the spirit or whoever it was and received at times the most emphatic answers. A cake of soap on the washstand was lifted and thrown heavily onto a china jug standing on the floor with such force that the soap was deeply marked. All of us were at the other side of the room when this happened. Our questions which we asked out loud were answered by raps apparently made on the back of a mirror in the room and it must be remembered though that no medium or spiritualist was present.

THE WHITE HOUSE

When the tour guides in Washington, DC, talk of the White House being haunted by the ghosts of former US presidents they are not speaking metaphorically, neither are they being melodramatic. It is known that Eleanor Roosevelt held séances in the White House during the Second World War and she claimed to be in contact with the spirit of Abraham Lincoln. During the Roosevelt residency their guest Queen Wilhelmina of the Netherlands was awoken in the night by a knock on her bedroom door. Thinking that it might be Eleanor Roosevelt she got out of bed, put on her nightgown and opened the door. There, framed in the doorway and looking as large as life, was the ghost of Abe Lincoln. Queen Wilhelmina's reaction is not recorded.

Winston Churchill was a frequent visitor to the White House during the Second World War and he often indulged in a hot bath, together with a cigar and a glass of whisky. One evening he climbed out of the bath and went into the adjoining bedroom to look for a towel when he noticed a man standing by the fireplace. It was Abraham Lincoln. Unperturbed, Churchill apologized for his state of undress: 'Good evening, Mr. President. You seem to have me at a disadvantage.' Lincoln is said to have smiled and tactfully withdrawn.

The wife of President Calvin Coolidge entertained guests to the White House with her recollections of the day she entered the Oval Office and saw Lincoln looking out across the Potomac with his hands clasped behind his back – a habit he acquired during the Civil War. Lincoln himself was a firm believer in the afterlife and enthusiastically participated in séances during his tenure in office prior to his assassination in 1865. He confided to his wife that he had a premonition of his own death. He dreamt that he was walking through the White House when he heard the sound of weeping coming from the East Room. When he entered he saw an open coffin surrounded by mourners and guarded by a detachment of Union soldiers. He asked one of the guards who it was who lay in the coffin, to be told, 'The President. He was killed by an assassin.' Lincoln then approached the coffin and saw his own corpse.

President Harry Truman often complained that he was prevented from working by Lincoln's ghost who would repeatedly knock on his door when he was attempting to draft an important speech. Truman wasn't known for his sense of humour and no one would have thought of playing practical jokes during his tenure in the Oval Office so it is assumed he was in earnest.

In the 1960s, Jacqueline Kennedy admitted that she had sensed Lincoln's presence on more than one occasion and 'took great comfort in it'. It is thought that Lincoln's ghost might be drawn to the White House because his son Willie died there and it is reported that the son has himself been seen wandering the corridors in search of his father.

ALCATRAZ

Long before Alcatraz Island in San Francisco Bay was converted into a prison to house America's most notorious criminals, the Native Americans warned the US army not to build a fortress on 'The Rock' as it was the dwelling place of evil spirits. Needless to say, their warnings were ignored. When the fortress was converted into a military prison in 1912, several soldiers were said to have been driven insane by mysterious noises in the night, by cold spots which turned their breath to mist even on warm summer evenings and by the sight of two burning red eyes which appeared in the cells on the lower level.

By 1934, the spirits had company when the Rock re-opened for business to house the most notorious gangsters of the prohibition era including 'Scarface' Al Capone and Machine Gun Kelly. But even the most hardened inmates feared being thrown into 'the hole', the windowless cells of D Block where the red-eyed demon was said to be waiting to consume lost souls.

On one memorable night during the 1940s a prisoner was hurled screaming into solitary in 14D and continued yelling until early the next morning. When the guards finally opened his cell, they found him dead with distinctive marks around his throat. An autopsy was conducted and the official cause of death was determined to be 'non self-inflicted strangulation'. The story gets more extraordinary when, according to the sworn statement of an eyewitness, the prisoners were lined up for roll-call the next morning and the number didn't tally. There was one extra prisoner in the line. So a guard walked along the line looking at each face to see if one of the inmates was playing a trick on him. He came face to face with the dead man who had been strangled in the night and who promptly vanished before his eyes. The guard later related this story to others and swore on the life of his children that it was true.

Despite the Warden's boast that the prison was escape-proof, several inmates tried to break out and died in the attempt. Their ghosts are said to haunt the hospital block where their bodies were taken. Other parts of the prison are host to the unquiet spirits of the five suicides and eight murders which took place before the prison was closed in 1963.

Since the Rock opened to tourists, visitors have claimed to have seen cell doors closing by themselves and to have heard the sound of sobbing, moaning and phantom footsteps, the screams of prisoners being beaten as well as the delirious cries of those made ill or driven insane by their confinement. Others have spoken of seeing phantom soldiers and prisoners pass along the corridors and out through solid walls, and many have complained of being watched even though the corridors and cells were empty.

Those brave enough to try out one of the bunks for size have found themselves pinned down by a weight on their chest as the previous occupant made his presence known and showed his resentment at having his privacy invaded. In the lower cells, 12 and 14 in particular, even the least sensitive tourists have admitted to picking up feelings of despair, panic and pain, and they have excused themselves to catch a breath of fresh air. Whenever a thermometer has been placed in cell 14D it has consistently measured between 20–30 degrees colder than the other cells in that block.

And what of the Rock's most notorious inmate, 'Scarface' Capone? Well, Capone may have been a 'big shot' on the outside but in the 'big house' he was apparently a model prisoner who sat quietly on his bunk in cell B206 learning to play the banjo. It is said that if you sit quietly in that cell you can hear the ghostly strains of Capone whiling away eternity playing popular tunes of the Roaring 20s.

THE EDGAR ALLAN POE HOUSE

The spirit of Edgar Allan Poe, author of *The Fall of the House of Usher* and other tales of terror, haunts both American fiction and the house in Baltimore where he lived as a young man in the 1830s. The narrow two and a half-storey brick house at 203 North Amity Street in an impoverished area is said to be so spooky that even local gangs are scared to break in. When the police arrived to investigate a reported burglary in 1968 they saw a phantom light in the ground floor window floating up to reappear on the second floor and then in the attic, but when they entered the property there was no one to be seen.

Even in daylight the house is unsettling. An eerie

portrait of Poe's wife, painted as she lay in her coffin, hangs in one room, her melancholic gaze following visitors around the room. Local residents have also reported seeing a shadowy figure working at a desk at a second floor window, although Poe, whose morbid obsession with premature burial led to his incarceration in an asylum, worked in the attic.

The curator has recorded many incidents of poltergeist activity and this appears to originate in the bedroom that belonged to Poe's grandmother. Here, doors and windows have opened and closed by themselves, visitors have been tapped on the shoulder and disembodied voices have been heard. Psychic investigators have also reported seeing a stout, grey-haired old woman dressed in clothing of the period gliding through the rooms.

In a twist of which the master of the macabre might have been perversely proud, local parents still use the spectre of the horror writer to terrify their children into doing what they are told. Poe has become the bogeyman of Baltimore.

TOYS "R" US

It is a common misconception that ghosts only inhabit crumbling castles and mouldering mansions. The modern Toys "R" Us superstore in Sunnyvale, California occupies a substantial plot on what had been a ranch and an apple orchard back in the nineteenth century. It is assumed that the poltergeist activity that has been witnessed there is connected with the previous owner John Murphy who, it appears, disliked children, as well as the commercial development of his former home.

Each morning, employees arrive to find stock scattered across the floor and items placed on the wrong shelves. Turnover in staff increased when sensitive staff members heard a voice calling their name and were then touched by invisible hands. The fragrant scent of fresh flowers has unsettled several employees, but it was the unwanted attentions of a phantom who assaulted female staff in the ladies' washroom which brought the matter to the attention of the local press and ghost buffs around the globe in 1978.

As a result, local journalist Antoinette May and psychic Sylvia Brown camped out in the store overnight with a photographer and a number of ghost catchers. Once the staff had left for the night and the lights were dimmed, Sylvia began to sense a male presence approaching the group. In her mind's eye she 'saw' a tall, thin man striding down the aisle towards her with his hands in his pockets. In her head she heard him speak with a Swedish accent, identifying himself as Johnny Johnson and warning her that she would get wet if she stayed where she was. It later emerged that a well had existed on that spot. Sylvia established such a strong connection with Johnson that she was able to draw out his life history. He had come to California in the mid-1800s from Pennsylvania where he had worked as a preacher before succumbing to an inflammation of the brain which affected his behaviour. This appears to account for his antics in the aisles and the ladies' washroom, as well as the nickname 'Crazy Johnny', given to him by locals at the time.

Johnny lived out his later years working as a ranch hand for John Murphy, pining for a woman named Elizabeth Tafee who broke his heart when she left him to marry a lawyer. Johnny was 80 when he died from loss of blood after an accident with an axe while chopping wood.

Infra-red photographs taken for Arthur Myers' book on the haunting, *The Ghostly Register*, appear to show the figure of a man in the aisles of the store. Surprisingly, the publicity surrounding the haunting hasn't put off the customers, and it has allayed the fears of the employees who are no longer upset by the disturbances – they now know it's only 'Crazy Johnny'.

CHAPTER 7

Spooky sites

Unquiet spirits rarely linger in graveyards
as they do not wish to be reminded of
how they died. Some may even be unaware that
they are dead.

I n three days of fighting at the battle of Gettysburg in July 1863, a battle that was to mark the turning point in the American Civil War, 53,000 men lost their lives. The scale of the slaughter surpassed even that of the bloodiest days on the Somme during the First World War. No wonder then that visitors to the site have sworn that they have seen spectral soldiers wandering the battlefield as disorientated as the day they were killed. Some say it is the most haunted place in America.

HAUNTED HOTEL

On the first day of the battle rebel snipers were able to pick off retreating Union soldiers from their vantage point in the Farnsworth House on Baltimore Pike. The house, still pockmarked with bullet holes, is now a small hotel where guests have awoken in the night to find an indistinct figure at the end of their bed. Odder still was the occasion when a local radio station set up an outside broadcast from the Farnsworth House only to have the power and telephone lines cut out. A local psychic, who was on site to give impressions to the listeners, heard disembodied voices warning their comrades that 'traitors' were around and he suddenly realized that the sound engineers were dressed in blue shirts and blue jeans – the same colour as the Union uniforms of the Civil War.

Several tourists have approached the park rangers over the years to ask the identity of a ragged, barefooted man dressed in a butternut shirt and trousers with a large floppy hat who appears at the rock formation known as the Devil's Den. He always says the same thing, 'What you're looking for is over there,' while pointing north-east towards the Plum Run, then promptly vanishes. The description fits that of the Texans who were a ragbag unit feared for their fighting spirit.

At the wooded end of the Triangular Field, site of Colonel Chamberlain's heroic bayonet charge which drove Confederate troops off the hill known as Little Round Top, visitors have documented chaotic paranormal activity including phantom musket fire and drum rolls. Shadowy rebel sharpshooters have been seen taking cover among the trees, but whenever the ghost hunters enter the field to record these phantom figures their cameras malfunction. There appears to be some form of electromagnetic disturbance hanging like a pall over the field; even photographs of the area taken from the outside looking in are either fogged or fail to develop. One possible explanation is that it is a mass of residual personal energy discharged into the atmosphere following the violent death of so many soldiers.

Several visitors have regaled their fellow travellers with tales of having heard musket fire from Little Round Top and even having smelt acrid clouds of cordite and cannon smoke. In fact, it is known that on the third day of the battle the sound of the massed cannons was so loud that it could be heard in Washington, 80 miles away. But the most unearthly episode must have been that experienced by a group of volunteer re-enactors who worked as extras on the epic recreation of the battle for the movie Gettysburg in 1993. During a break in the filming the group were admiring the sunset from Little Round Top when a grizzled old man approached them in the uniform of a Union private. He smelt of sulphur which was used in gunpowder of the period and his uniform was threadbare and scorched, unlike those of the extras. The man handed out spare rounds and commented on the fury of the battle. It was only later when they showed the rounds to the armourer that they learnt these were authentic musket rounds from the period.

The battle was finally decided by a single suicidal assault, the infamous attack known as Pickett's Charge, in which 12,000 Confederate infantry marched shoulder to shoulder across an open field only to be massacred by massed cannons and musket fire. In that single, fatal hour 10,000 were killed and with them died General Robert E.

Lee's hopes of victory. Park rangers have witnessed many apparitions in the field after visiting hours including an unidentified mounted officer and another who was the image of General Lee. Local residents have maintained that on warm summer evenings they have encountered cold spots while out walking which transformed their breath to mist.

THE TOWN TOO TOUGH TO DIE

They called Tombstone, Arizona, 'The Town Too Tough To Die' and it appears that certain of its most notorious inhabitants are equally reluctant to go quietly. The town is now preserved as a national museum with many of the old buildings lovingly restored to their former rickety glory and stocked with original artefacts from its violent past including the hearse that transported bodies to Boot Hill, the hangman's noose and the honky-tonk piano which accompanied many a barroom brawl. Some say that if you stay after closing time you can hear the piano playing 'Red River Valley', the cowboys' favourite tune and hear the echo of their raucous laughter.

Some of the meanest gunfighters of the old West did their hardest drinking and gambling in the town's notorious Bird Cage Theatre which took its name from the 14 cribs suspended from the ceiling in which 'painted ladies', dressed in exotic feathers, would swing. The Bird Cage also served as a saloon where the cowboys and card sharps took their pleasure with women who could out-drink and out-cuss the best of them. Arguments were settled with a six gun and the loser was buried on Boot Hill, so named because many of its residents died with their boots on.

The streets of Tombstone were the setting for numerous showdowns, the most famous being the gunfight at the OK Corral when Marshall Wyatt Earp, his brothers and their consumptive trigger-happy friend Doc Holliday faced down the Clanton and McLaury gang, three of whom were killed. In the aftermath, the surviving Clantons and their friends took their bloody revenge. Virgil Earp was shot in the back while playing pool in the Bird Cage and his dying words are said to echo there after dark.

The tour guides are fond of telling visitors that as many as 31 ghosts are thought to haunt the saloon which was the site of 26 killings – a fact borne out by the 140 bullet holes that can be seen peppering the ceiling. The spook most frequently seen in the saloon is a stage hand dressed in black striped trousers, wearing a card dealer's visor and carrying a clipboard. He is said to appear from nowhere, walk across the stage and exit through the facing wall. Tourists have also reported seeing the ghost of a young boy who had died of yellow fever in 1882 and heard an unidentified woman sighing plaintively as if pining for her lost love. Others have commented on how impressed they have been by the authenticity of the actors' clothes in the gambling parlour and the dancehall, only to be told that the museum doesn't employ actors, nor does it ask its staff to dress in period costumes.

Since it is a museum, no one is allowed to smoke inside

the buildings but nevertheless visitors will often remark on the strong smell of cigar smoke which lingers round the card tables and some have spoken of the delicate scent of lilac perfume in the backstage bathroom. Equally odd is the $100 poker chip which mysteriously appeared on the poker table one day then promptly vanished after being locked away in a desk before turning up in a filing cabinet some days later. And this is not the only object which appears and disappears to the bewilderment of the museum staff. The ghosts seem to enjoy playing hide and seek with small but significant items which they know the staff will notice if they are missing or out of place. Furniture has moved by itself and one member of the museum staff was physically attacked by a mischievous spirit who hit the tour guide on the back of the knee causing him to fall to the floor. Anyone who doubts that there is a physical presence in the old saloon only has to put his hand in the notorious 'cold spot' and feel the contrast with the warm air surrounding it to sense a distinct chill in the atmosphere.

Over the years several ghost hunters have attempted to capture the ghosts on film, but their cameras have malfunctioned as if triggered by an influx of energy as ghosts appear. Unattended still cameras have fired off exposures by themselves and have altered focus in the middle of shooting before resetting themselves correctly. However, it seems the ghosts can register on electrical equipment if their emission is strong enough. Small balls of light have been captured on film floating up from the floor and a face has been seen in the large painting which hangs behind the bar. One female member of staff who works in the gift shop on the ground floor of the Bird Cage Theatre swears she once saw on a security monitor a lady in a white dress walking through the cellar at closing time when all the visitors had left.

TOMBSTONE'S SPOOKY SITES

Other haunted sites in Tombstone include Nellie Cashman's Restaurant, where customers and employees have reported seeing dishes crash to the floor, and Schiefflin Hall where rowdy town council meetings were held in the 1880s. At the Wells Fargo stage stop ghostly drivers and phantom passengers have been seen alighting from a spectral stagecoach on their way to the Grand Hotel – renamed Big Nose Kate's after its most famous owner, a prostitute who enjoyed a volatile relationship with its most famous resident, Doc Holliday, who lived in room 201. Residents and tourists have also reported seeing a man in a black frock coat who starts walking across the street but never appears on the other side and traffic often stops for a woman in white who committed suicide after her child died of fever in the 1880s.

The town's tour guides thought they had heard and seen it all until recently when they were shown photographs taken by visitors on two separate occasions. Both were taken at the same spot on Boot Hill and at first sight they appeared to be typical snapshots of their relatives standing in front of the gravestones, but on closer inspection the first subject was shadowed by the faint but unmistakable image of a cowboy in period costume. However, there was nothing discernible of this phantom figure below the knee. In the second shot, taken by someone unconnected with the first tourist, their friend or family member smiled from the photo unaware that behind them could be seen a ghostly pair of cowboy boots and the lower part of their owner in precisely the spot where the legless cowboy had been seen in the first photograph. It may be that the film or exposure setting on the first camera was less sensitive to residual personal energy and so captured the cowboy's upper half which would be the stronger emanation, while the second camera captured the fainter portion only.

A GLIMPSE INTO THE PAST

For over a century, tourists have been allowed access to enjoy the elegant palace and gardens of Versailles, near Paris, where Louis XVI and his queen Marie Antoinette lived in splendour just prior to the French Revolution. However, few can have seen as much of the palace's past glories as Eleanor Jourdain and Anne Moberly did in the summer of 1901.

Miss Moberly, aged 55, was the head of a women's residential hall at Oxford University and 35-year-old Miss Jourdain had been offered a post as her assistant. It had been Miss Jourdain's idea to invite Miss Moberley to spend part of the summer vacation touring France with her in the hope of becoming better acquainted while she considered the offer. Both were the daughters of Anglican clerics and not given to a belief in the supernatural, but what they saw on their visit to Versailles on 10 August shook their faith and forced them to question their beliefs.

They began with a tour of the main palace and then decided to walk to the Petit Trianon, one of two smaller palatial buildings in the grounds where the ill-fated Marie Antoinette retreated to escape the formalities of the court. It was a warm day with barely a cloud in the sky, cooled by a soft freshening breeze – ideal walking weather, in fact – but after strolling through a large formal garden and a glade the ladies lost their way. Perhaps they had been distracted in the course of conversation, or had misread their guidebook, but whatever the reason, they now found themselves at the Grand Trianon, the palace built for Louis XIV.

Unperturbed, they consulted their Baedeker guide, which offered an alternative route to the smaller building by way of a lane which lay ahead of them. Neither lady remarked on the fact that they appeared to be the only visitors in this part of the grounds, although it struck them both as very strange considering how popular Versailles was with tourists at that time of the season. But Miss Jourdain did think it odd when her companion did not take the opportunity to ask directions from a domestic servant who was leaning out of the window of a building shaking the dust from a bed sheet. It later transpired that the older woman had not seen the servant. In fact, when they compared notes some months later they discovered that their shared experience differed in small but significant details.

The end of the lane divided into three paths and it

was here that the English visitors came upon two men dressed in green coats and three-cornered hats whom they assumed were gardeners. One of the men offered directions in such a gruff, offhand manner that Miss Jourdain felt the need to ask again, but she received the same response. Looking around for a more civil guide she caught sight of a woman and a young girl standing in the doorway of a cottage and thought it odd that they should be dressed in such old-fashioned clothes. She later learnt that Miss Moberly had not commented on it because she hadn't seen the women – nor, for that matter, had she seen the cottage.

It was at this point that both women began to sense a change in the atmosphere. They were overcome by a profound sense of melancholy and a detachment from reality as if they were sleepwalking through a particularly lucid dream. Miss Moberly was later to describe the atmosphere as 'unnatural' and distinctly 'unpleasant': ' . . . even the trees behind the building seemed to have become flat and lifeless, like a wood worked in tapestry.

There were no effects of light and shade, and no wind stirred the trees. It was all intensely still.'

The atmosphere was unusually oppressive as they came to the edge of a wood in front of which was a pillared kiosk, intended perhaps for tired visitors who wished to sit and shield themselves from the sun. But neither lady felt disposed to do so when they caught sight of the face of a man in a cloak who was seated nearby. Both women sensed a shiver of repulsion as they looked on the swarthy, malevolent features. But was he looking at them or through them? Neither said a word, but instead debated whether to take the left or right-hand path. While they were considering what to do a handsome looking young man, his face framed in black ringlets, appeared in period costume complete with buckle shoes, a cloak and wide-brimmed hat and he advised them to take the path to the right through the wood. An instant later he was gone, but his directions had proven correct. As they emerged from the trees they saw the Petit Trianon in the clearing and approached it with a palpable sense of relief. It was then that Miss Moberly spotted a rather pretty fair-haired young woman in period costume sketching near the terrace. She was attired in a low cut white dress with a full skirt, a light coloured scarf around her shoulders and a wide-brimmed hat to shield her pale skin from the sun. There was something about this artist that predisposed Miss Moberly to dislike the woman, but she couldn't put her feelings into words. Curiously, her companion made no comment as they passed and it was only weeks later that Miss Jourdain admitted that she hadn't seen anyone sketching in the garden. The oppressive stillness returned as they toured the outside of the house but swiftly evaporated when they encountered a French wedding party in modern dress near the entrance whom they joined for a tour of the rooms.

SENSE OF FOREBODING

Neither lady spoke of their experience until a week later

when Miss Moberly was overcome with the same stifling sense of foreboding that she had sensed at the kiosk while recalling her experiences in a letter to her sister. At this she turned to Miss Jourdain and asked if the younger woman thought that the palace might be haunted. 'Yes I do,' replied Miss Jourdain. The two women then shared their recollections of that day. It was only later that they learnt that 10 August had been a significant day in French history for it was the day that revolutionaries marched on Versailles and seized the royal family. Had the two women unconsciously tapped into a residual memory of that pivotal day in the minds of those who had been present and sensed the approaching threat? And could it have been Marie Antoinette herself that Miss Moberly had seen sketching in the garden of the Petit Trianon? Miss Jourdain determined that another visit to Versailles was called for. Her second outing proved no less remarkable.

On a chilly damp day in January 1902 she returned to Versailles and immediately set off in search of the Hameau, a model peasant village where Marie

Antoinette had amused herself play-acting an idyllic rustic life with her friends. As she neared the site Miss Jourdain was again overcome with a sense of unreality, as if she was sleepwalking through someone else's dream. When she came in sight of the Hameau she passed two labourers in hooded cloaks who were gathering lopped branches and loading them into a cart. When she turned to observe them more closely they had gone. In the model village she was overwhelmed by an oppressive atmosphere and was tempted to turn back, but decided to press on as she suspected this might be her last opportunity to get to the bottom of the mystery. Eventually she emerged into a wooded park where she wandered a labyrinth of paths screened by dense hedges. The only person she saw there was an elderly gardener, but she heard the rustle of silk dresses which she thought impractical in wet weather and overheard the excited chatter of women speaking French. Occasionally she thought she could hear faint strains of chamber music although there were no musicians in sight. On returning to the main palace she asked the tour guides if there were any actors on the grounds in historical costume, or musicians, and was informed that there were neither.

Determined to verify what they had seen, Miss Jourdain and Miss Moberly embarked on a thorough examination of all the documents they could find relating to the palace during the period immediately prior to the Revolution. What they found appeared to validate their experiences. They traced a plan of the grounds which showed a cottage precisely where Miss Jourdain had said she had seen it, although nothing remained by 1901. They also found proof that there had been a pillared kiosk at the spot where they had observed the malevolent looking man who answered the description of the Comte de Vaudreuil. He had betrayed the queen by fooling her into permitting the staging of an anti-royalist play which had incited disaffected elements within the court to join the revolutionaries. As for the costumed figures, they identified the men in the three-cornered hats and green coats as Swiss Guards and the young man with black curls who had offered directions near the kiosk as the messenger who had hurried to warn the queen of a mob marching on the palace. This incident occurred on 5 October 1789, the same day that a cart had been hired to carry firewood from the park near the Hameau. If Miss Moberly and Miss Jourdain had indeed tuned in to this particular day it would explain why all the men they had seen on that hot day in August were dressed in autumnal clothes and why the two women had been oppressed by a sense of foreboding.

PUBLISHED, AND DAMNED

Convinced that they had experienced a genuine glimpse into the past – a phenomenon known as retrocognition – the two ladies decided to publish their story. The resulting account, modestly titled *An Adventure* (1911), became an instant sensation and has remained a hotly debated issue ever since. Sceptics have argued that the women had mistaken actors in period costume for genuine spectres and in evidence of this offer Phillipe Jullian's biography of turn of the century poet Robert de Montesquiou. Jullian notes that de Montesquiou and his friends often amused themselves by dressing in period costume and rehearsing historical plays in the grounds of Versailles and that Marie Antoinette was a prominent character. Although a perfectly rational scenario, this does not explain why Miss Jourdain did not see the domestic servant shaking a cloth from the window or the lady sketching in the garden, both of whom were observed by Miss Moberly. Neither does it explain the appearance of the woman and girl at the doorway of the cottage which had long been demolished, nor does it account for the kiosk which had also gone by 1901. Miss Moberly and Miss Jourdain were equally adamant that the handsome young messenger and the men collecting fallen branches had vanished within moments of being seen and could not have moved on in so short a time.

Unfortunately both women naively willed the copyright to a sceptical friend, art historian Dame Joan Evans, who subscribed to Phillipe Jullian's rational explanation of events. Consequently, Dame Joan Evans refused to allow the book to be reprinted after the authors' death, but a century later their story continues to be cited as one of the most compelling cases of retrocognition.

Such episodes are very rare, but perhaps they are not as uncommon as one might imagine. In 1926, two English ladies shared a similar experience. They took a walking tour of the villages near their new home to familiarize themselves with the area when they came upon a large Georgian house in substantial grounds surrounded by a wall. But when they made enquiries as to the owner and its history none of the locals knew which house they were talking about. Intrigued, on their next outing the ladies retraced their steps but found only a vacant plot with no sign of the house.

THE GHOSTS OF GLASTONBURY

Glastonbury is one of the most sacred and mysterious

sites in Britain, and of great spiritual significance to mystically minded Christians and pagans alike. Legend has it that King Arthur and Queen Guinevere are buried within the ruins of Glastonbury Abbey and that the Holy Grail, the chalice from which Jesus is said to have drunk on the night before his crucifixion, is hidden nearby. But of all the legends associated with Glastonbury the most extraordinary and controversial is that concerning the discovery of the ruins of the abbey itself.

In 1907, architect and archaeologist Frederick Bligh Bond (1864–1945) was appointed director of excavations by the Church of England and charged with the task of unearthing the abbey ruins which several previous incumbents had spent their lives searching for in vain. The work was unpaid, but Bligh had a thriving architectural practice in Bristol and he viewed the search for the abbey as an almost mystical mission. He was confident that he would succeed where the others had failed for he believed that he had an uncommon advantage over his predecessors.

His interest in paranormal phenomena had led him to join the Society for Psychical Research through which he had met Captain John Allen Bartlett, an eager advocate of automatic writing. Together the two men took up pen and paper in the hope of pinpointing the location of the ruins by tapping into what Jung had called the Collective Unconscious. The quality of the messages they received swiftly persuaded them that they were in communication with separate discarnate personalities, quite possibly the ghosts of long dead monks who had lived in the monastery.

At the first session, which took place in November 1907, the two men sat opposite each other across an empty table in reverent expectation. Bartlett took the part of the medium and Bond the 'sitter'. This involved Bond asking the questions while placing two fingers on the back of Bartlett's hand to connect with the spirits.

'Can you tell us anything about Glastonbury,' asked the architect, to which an invisible force answered in a legible scrawl by animating Bartlett's hand:

'All knowledge is eternal and is available to mental sympathy.'

The connection had been made and information as to the location of the chapels and other buried structures was freely given in a mixture of Latin and English by a disembodied spirit who identified himself as a fifteenth-century monk named Brother William (possibly William of Malmesbury).

To Bond and Bartlett's delight the 'monk' and his companions, known as 'The Watchers', supplied very detailed information regarding the location of the abbey's foundations. When the excavations started, often the workmen would simply have to dig a few feet down to hit the precise spot, after which the archaeologists would move in and begin sifting the soil for artefacts. Needless to say, Bond's benefactors were beside themselves and the full extent of the ancient site was revealed over dozens of sessions during the next five years.

By 1917, Bond felt justly proud in having uncovered one of Britain's most sacred sites and decided to tell his story in print. But when *The Gates of Remembrance* was published in 1918, the Church condemned it and strenuously denied that anything other than conventional methods had been used to unearth the abbey. In an effort to distance themselves from Bond they terminated his employment, banned him from ever setting foot within the grounds again and ordered that his guidebook to Glastonbury be removed from the shelves of the gift shop.

Since that time the occult significance of the abbey's location has been argued over by scholars who believe that it was intentionally built on an ancient pagan site to conform to an alignment of stars. Bond's communications with 'Brother William' appear to confirm this.

'. . . *our Abbey was a message in ye stones. In ye foundations and ye distances be a mystery – the mystery of our faith, which ye have forgotten and we also in ye latter days.*

All ye measurements were marked plain on ye slabbes in Mary's Chappel, and ye have destroyed them. So it was recorded, as they who builded and they who came after knew aforehand where they should build. But these things are overpast and of no value now. The spirit was lost and with the loss of the spirit the body decayed and was of no use to (us).

There was the Body of Christ, and round him would have been the Four Ways. Two were builded and no more. In ye floor of ye Mary Chappel was ye Zodiac, that all might see and understand the mystery. In ye midst of ye chappel he was laid; and the Cross of Hym who was our Example and Exemplar.'

GHOSTS OF THE LONDON UNDERGROUND

The London Underground, or the Tube as it is known to the commuters who use it, shuts down not long after midnight, which is a likely relief to its many late-night workers. Many employees fear they will meet more than muggers, drug addicts and drunks if they work the 'graveyard shift'.

When the original underground tunnels were excavated during the Victorian era several historic graveyards were destroyed to make way for the network, and it is believed that their inhabitants were none too pleased at having their eternal rest disturbed. Other historic sites including gaols, pauper's graves and, most significantly, seventeenth-century plague pits were wilfully destroyed in the name of progress. During the construction of St Pancras Station the church complained that the reburying of caskets at the site of an old cemetery was being carried out in haste and with disrespect for the dead. As recently as the 1960s the construction of the new Victoria line had to be delayed when a boring machine tore through a plague pit unearthing the corpses and traumatizing several brawny navvies.

If you add to this the number of poor souls who have committed suicide by throwing themselves under trains and those who have perished in disasters, you have a real-life ghost train experience waiting for the unwary traveller.

Aldwych

This station was built on the site of the Royal Strand Theatre and was said to be haunted by the ghost of an actress who hungers for applause. Closed in 1994, Aldwych had a higher than average turnover of cleaning and maintenance staff as dozens refused to work there after being confronted by a 'figure' which suddenly appeared on the tracks inside one of the approach tunnels without warning.

Bank

When Bank station was built, workmen are said to have disturbed the restless spirit of Sarah Whitehead, known locally as the 'Black Nun'. In life she was the sister of a bank cashier who had been executed for forgery in 1811. She acquired her nickname from the commuters who saw her dressed in black waiting, every evening for 40 years until her death, outside the bank where he had worked.

Covent Garden

Staff at Covent Garden demanded a transfer to another station in the 1950s after a tall Edwardian gentleman in a frock coat, top hat and wearing opera gloves appeared unannounced in their rest room. It is thought that he might be the actor William Terriss who was stabbed to death outside the Adelphi Theatre in the Strand in 1897. The station was built on the site of a bakery which the actor patronized en route to rehearsals.

Elephant & Castle

After closing time, when the station falls silent, the night staff have reported hearing phantom steps, inexplicable rapping sounds and doors banging shut. It is believed the platforms are haunted by the ghost of a traveller who was in such haste that he tripped and fell under an oncoming train.

Farringdon

Of all the London Underground stations, Farringdon is the one to avoid if you are travelling alone. It is the haunt of the 'Screaming Spectre', a vengeful young apprentice hat maker who was murdered in 1758 by her master and his daughter.

Highgate

Highgate underground station is in the vicinity of the famous cemetery of the same name, a place that guarantees some serious spectral activity. Contrary to popular belief, ghosts do not linger around their graves as they do not want to be reminded that they are dead or how they met their end. Instead they 'commute' to where they can relive their routine lives and for many recently deceased Londoners this means their home, office and the Tube network. And you thought the trains were overcrowded with the living!

Curiously, local residents claim to be able to hear the sound of trains running through an abandoned and overgrown cutting that was intended to connect with the Northern line when the station was extended in 1941.

South Kensington

The only reported sighting of a ghost train was made by a passenger in December 1928. The commuter claimed to have heard the screech of its brakes and to have seen a phantom figure dressed in an Edwardian smoking jacket and peaked cap clinging to the side of the engine just moments before it was swallowed up in the darkness of the tunnel.

GHOST FLIGHT

Executives of American carrier Eastern Airlines were literally haunted by their past when they decided to reuse parts salvaged from a crashed Tristar Lockheed L-1011 to repair other planes in their fleet. Their troubles began in December 1972 when Flight 401 fell out of the sky over the Florida Everglades claiming more than 100 lives including the pilot, Bob Loft, and flight engineer, Don Repo.

Within months of the crash, members of the cabin crew were reporting sightings of both men on their flights and these were augmented by sightings from passengers who had been disturbed by faint but full-length figures, subsequently identified as Loft and Repo from their photographs. One female passenger became hysterical when she saw the man in the seat next to her disappear. He had looked so pale and listless that she had called an attendant to see if he was ill. The attendant arrived just in time to see the man disappear before her eyes. He had been dressed in an Eastern Airlines uniform and was later identified from photographs as Don Repo.

On several occasions the pair have taken an active interest in the flight. A flight engineer was half way through a pre-flight check when Repo appeared and assured him that the inspection had already been carried out. One particularly persuasive account was recorded by a vice president of Eastern Airlines who had been enjoying a conversation with the captain of his Miamibound flight from JFK until he recognized the man as Bob Loft. Needless to say, the apparitions played havoc with the schedules. When the captain and two flight attendants saw Loft fade before their eyes they hastily cancelled the flight.

Usually the pair appear simply to check that all is well but on one particular flight they intervened to prevent a potentially fatal accident. Flight attendant Faye Merryweather swore she saw Repo looking inside an infrared oven in the galley and called the flight engineer and the co-pilot for assistance. The engineer immediately recognized Repo's face, then they heard him say, 'Watch out for fire on this airplane.' The warning proved timely. During the flight the aeroplane developed serious engine trouble and was forced to land short of its destination. The oven was subsequently replaced to appease the cabin crew who were becoming increasingly unsettled by such incidents.

This and other episodes are a matter of record in the files of the Flight Safety Foundation and the Federal Aviation

Agency. The former investigated several incidents and concluded: 'The reports were given by experienced and trustworthy pilots and crew. We consider them significant. The appearance of the dead flight engineer [Repo] . . . was confirmed by the flight engineer.'

The airline responded to the intensifying interest in their planes by refusing to co-operate with anyone other than the airline authorities. It appears they have learnt the true meaning of 'false economy'. The story inspired a bestselling book, *The Ghost of Flight 401*, by John G. Fuller and a 1978 TV movie of the same name starring Ernest Borgnine and the then unknown Kim Basinger.

HAUNTED HOLLYWOOD

'What the average man calls Death, I believe to be merely the beginning of Life itself. We simply live beyond the shell. We emerge from out of its narrow confines like a chrysalis. Why call it Death? Or, if we give it the name Death, why surround it with dark fears and sick

imaginings? I am not afraid of the Unknown.'
Rudolph Valentino

Living legends die hard, particularly those whose larger-than-life personalities dominated the silver screen in Hollywood's heyday. Hollywood Memorial Cemetery (recently renamed Hollywood Forever) is the oldest graveyard in Tinseltown and is reputed to be uncommonly active as far as spectral sightings are concerned. The cemetery backs on to Paramount Studios which is said to be haunted by the ghosts of its most enduring stars, Douglas Fairbanks and Rudolph Valentino, who do not seem content with merely revisiting the scene of their past glories. Curiously, the ghosts do not appear during the day while filming is taking place, but instead wait until the sound stages are quiet and the crew are preparing for the next day's shoot. The most remarkable incident occurred one evening when a technician fell 20 ft from a lighting gantry and was apparently saved from certain death by a spectral Samaritan who broke his fall. He seemed to hover in the air just inches from the ground for an instant, before dropping to the floor, unharmed, in full view of his startled colleagues.

On another occasion two property men suspected their colleagues of playing a practical joke after chairs that they had stacked in a corner of a storeroom mysteriously returned to the centre. They decided to stay overnight in the hope of catching whoever was responsible and that night, to their horror, they heard scraping sounds and saw the furniture moving around the room by itself. The following night they plucked up sufficient courage to attempt another vigil, but the phenomenon did not recur. Evidently the spirits were satisfied that their presence had been acknowledged.

At Culver City Studios, carpenters speak in whispers of a grey figure dressed in a jacket and tie and sporting a fedora hat who walks right through them and disappears through a door in the facing wall. From the description he appears to be the restless spirit of former studio boss Thomas Ince who is credited with establishing the studio system and creating the role of the producer. He died in suspicious circumstances aboard a yacht owned by William Randolph Hearst in 1924. It is rumoured that the rabidly jealous newspaper tycoon was trying to shoot Charlie Chaplin at the time but killed Ince by mistake.

For a generation of silent movie fans Rudolph Valentino personified the 'Latin lover' and after his death at the age of 31 he became the most active ghost in Hollywood. His spirit glides elegantly through the rooms of his former mansion, the Falcon's Lair, gazing longingly from a second-floor window and visiting the horses in the stables. Staff at Paramount studios have sworn they have seen 'the Sheik' admiring the stock in the costume department and walking soundlessly through Studio Five where he lived every man's fantasy, seducing beautiful female film stars and being handsomely paid for doing so. Curiously, his fans appear equally persistent. The ghost of a lady admirer in a veil is often seen bringing phantom flowers to the star's tomb at the Hollywood Forever cemetery.

Another haunted studio is Universal which was the setting for the original silent version of *Phantom of the Opera* (1925) starring horror screen legend Lon Chaney Sr whose spirit has been seen scampering along the catwalks and gantries with his cape billowing behind. Chaney, who died in 1930, was known as 'the man of a thousand faces' because of his uncanny ability to transform himself – by aid of make up and acting – into all manner of the most hideously deformed characters.

TV's original Superman, actor George Reeves, is said to have shot himself at his Beverly Hills home in 1959, three days before his wedding, because he could not cope with being typecast. His friends and family maintain that he was murdered. Visitors to the house have reported sensing his apparition dressed in his Superman costume.

Another mysterious murder/suicide was that of Thelma Todd who appeared with silent comedy stars Laurel and Hardy, and Buster Keaton. She managed to make the transition to sound pictures but died in

1935 in the garage of her beachside café on the Pacific Coast Highway, near Malibu. The police suspected a suicide, but there were bloodstains which were never satisfactorily explained. The present owners of the property claim to have seen her ghost on the premises and to have smelt exhaust fumes in the empty garage.

The Vogue Theatre, Hollywood Boulevard, is said to be haunted by a projectionist who collapsed and died in the projection booth, a maintenance engineer, and a school teacher and her pupils who were burned to death when their school, Prospect Elementary, which had previously occupied the site, was destroyed in a blaze. The theatre had been a regular venue for studio broadcasts but there have been so many instances of (paranormal) interference with electrical equipment that TV companies are reluctant to hire the theatre any more.

Other haunted Hollywood locations include the Roosevelt Hotel in which several stars made their second home. Guests have frequently complained of hearing a clarinet playing in the early hours only to be told that it is the resident ghost of screen star Montgomery Clift who had stayed at the hotel during the filming of From Here To Eternity and had to learn the instrument to secure the role that earned him his third Academy Award nomination. Guests at the time had complained of the unsociable hours he chose to practise and they are continuing to complain long after his death.

More unsettling is the case of the haunted mirror which used to take pride of place in a room Marilyn Monroe had stayed in. Long after Marilyn's death a cleaner suffered the shock of seeing Monroe's face appear in the mirror, forcing the management to remove it and hang it in the hallway. But the ghost reappeared in the mirror whenever a guest paused to check their appearance and it has since acquired a reputation as 'the ghost glass'.

Some ghosts had too good a time during their life to waste the afterlife wailing and moaning. Writer, director and bon vivant Orson Welles continues to enjoy brandy and cigars at his favourite table in Sweet Lady Jane's

Restaurant in Hollywood. Fellow diners, the living ones that is, regularly comment on the smell of cigar smoke but the maître d'hôtel refuses to give a refund.

Actor Hugh Grant is said to have heard the ghost of Bette Davis sobbing and moaning as it sweeps through the luxury apartments in Los Angeles' Colonial Building where she used to live, while another larger-than-life actress, comedian Lucille Ball, is said to haunt her home at 100 North Roxbury Drive; windows have been broken in the Ball house, furniture has moved of its own accord and shouting has been traced to an empty attic. But if the new owners were thinking of calling in the Ghostbusters they might want to think again. *Ghostbuster* star Dan Ackroyd may have been fearless when facing spooky special effects on the big screen but in real life he admits to being unnerved when he realized he was sharing his bed with the ghost of Mama Cass Elliot, one time member of 60s group The Mamas and the Papas. 'A ghost certainly haunts my house. It once even crawled into bed with me. I rolled over and just nuzzled up to whatever it was and went back to sleep. The ghost also turns on the Stairmaster and moves jewellery across the dresser. I'm sure it's Mama Cass because you get the feeling it's a big ghost.'

One would imagine that behind the walls of their luxury homes Hollywood's celebrities would enjoy peace and privacy, but the home of actress Elke Sommer and husband Joe Hyams was a living hell to rival anything seen on screen in the *Amityville Horror*. On several occasions the couple and their dinner guests witnessed the spectre of a middle-aged man in a white suit passing through the rooms. The couple were repeatedly forced to flee from the choking fumes of fires which spontaneously and inexplicably broke out at all hours of day and night. Fire Department investigators made a thorough examination of the luxury property on several occasions with particular attention paid to the attic where the conflagrations had begun, but they could find no physical cause for the blazes such as faulty wiring, and expressed disbelief that the fires could have caught hold in that part of the house as there was no inflammable material to feed the flames. Dissatisfied, the couple called in the American Society for Psychical Research who documented a catalogue of anomalous incidents, but they could not appease the spirits. Sommer and Hyams were finally forced to sell their dream home before it burned down with them inside. It was subsequently sold no less than 15 times with many owners living there for less than a year.

But arguably the most disturbing Hollywood haunting was that experienced one evening in the 1960s by the late Sharon Tate, actress wife of film director Roman Polanski. Tate was in her bedroom when she saw the spectre of a 'creepy little man', as she later described him, enter her room and appear to search for something. She recognized him as the former owner of the house, Paul Burn, a theatrical agent who had shot himself in the upstairs bathroom after the break up of his marriage to actress Jean Harlow. When Tate fled from the room she came face to face with a second apparition at the foot of the stairs. It was the spirit of a woman who was tied to a pillar with her throat cut. Tate's screams echoed round the walls for it was her own ghost. Shortly afterwards the house became the scene of a sickening ritual murder when Tate was killed by members of the so-called 'Manson Family', who tied her to the staircase and slashed her throat.

THEIR FINAL BOW

Hollywood is not the only place to be haunted by dead celebrities whose egos were too large to go quietly. Flamboyant entertainer Liberace (1919–1987) reputedly haunts Carluccio's restaurant off the Las Vegas strip which he once owned and where he still demands that his presence is acknowledged. Regular customers recall the time when the lights failed and all power to the kitchen was cut off until someone remembered that it was Liberace's birthday. After they had drunk to his memory the power came back on. But unfortunately that is not the extent of his activities. Several female patrons swear they have been on the receiving end of the former owner's mischievous sense of humour – they claim to have been locked in the cubicles in the powder room by an unseen hand.

Elvis Presley, arguably the biggest star of all, is clearly not yet ready to bow out gracefully. Las Vegas stage hands have reported seeing the portly apparition in his trademark white sequined suit taking a final bow at the venue he made his own in the early 1970s, the Hilton hotel. Elvis has also been seen revisiting scenes of his former glory, specifically the former RCA recording studios off Nashville's Music Row where the mere mention of his name is answered by falling ladders, exploding light bulbs and odd noises echoing through the sound system.

Not all the apparitions in Las Vegas are those of the entertainers who lived like kings in the 24-hour pleasure palaces. The town's most notorious resident was Mobster 'Bugsy' Siegel who is credited with turning the desert town into the gambling capital of America.

On 20 June 1947, Bugsy was 'whacked' by disgruntled business associates who accused him of overspending their ill-gotten gains and skimming some off the top for himself. He has been sighted mooching about his favourite casino in the Flamingo Hotel in Vegas dressed in a smoking jacket and grinning from ear to ear, as well as in the presidential suite which he had made his home. He has also been spotted running and ducking to avoid imaginary bullets at his girlfriend's mansion in Beverly Hills, the scene of his murder, although he was shot while seated on the sofa. Perhaps it is his guilty conscience which pursues him into the afterlife.

SPOOKED CELEBRITIES

Some people can take spirits in their stride while others need to sleep for weeks afterwards with the light on. Oddly enough it's usually the action hero types who discover that their fearless on-screen persona deserts them when faced with the inexplicable.

Jean Claude Van Damme, 'the Muscles from Brussels', admits he was spooked the night he came face to face with a ghost in his bathroom mirror. 'I suddenly felt very cold. I turned round and thought: "I've had a vision or something." It was blue and white and had a very smoky body. Since that moment I've believed in ghosts.'

Movie star Nicolas Cage, who has cultivated an edgy, unpredictable screen persona in such films as *Face/Off*, *Windtalkers* and *Lord of War*, admits he was freaked by a phantom intruder at his uncle Francis Ford Coppola's home. 'I was living in the attic, and there were bats there between the walls – you could hear the scratching. One night I was not quite asleep when the door in front of my bed opened and there was this pitch-black silhouette of a woman with big hair. I thought it was my aunt coming to say goodnight. So I said, "Goodnight", and it didn't say anything. Then it moved towards me and my body froze up and I let out this bloodcurdling scream and threw my pillow at it. Then it disappeared. Now, am I saying I saw a ghost? I still don't know. But I saw something that freaked me out.'

The Matrix star Keanu Reeves may have been a messianic hero who saved the world in cyberspace, but he can still wake up in a sweat when haunted by nightmares of a real ghostly encounter during his childhood. 'I was living in New Jersey when I saw and felt this ghost. I remember just staring at this suit which had no body or legs in it as it came into the room before disappearing. It was a double-breasted suit in white, and I looked at my nanny who was just as shocked as me. I just couldn't get back to sleep afterwards, and I still see the figure in my dreams and nightmares.'

Richard Dreyfuss, star of *Jaws* and *Close Encounters of the Third Kind*, was wide awake when he encountered the spook that cured him of his cocaine habit. 'I had a car crash in the late 1970s, when I was really screwed up, and I started seeing these ghostly visions of a little girl every night. I couldn't shake this image. Every day it became clearer and I didn't know who the hell she was. I had no kids, I was a bachelor. Then I realized that kid was either the child I didn't kill the night I smashed up my car, or it was the daughter that I didn't have yet. I immediately sobered up. I still don't get it, but, hey, it did the trick.'

LIFE IMITATING ART

Even horror movie queens are unnerved when they meet the real thing as *Scream* star Neve Campbell discovered when she bought her Hollywood home without checking its history. 'Someone was murdered in my house six years before I bought it. I had friends round and I left them in the living room to go in the kitchen and they both thought I had just walked back in again. But I hadn't, so what they saw was the woman who was murdered. The previous owner had an exorcist come in, but I don't think it worked.'

Rumour has it that celebrity ex-couple Ethan Hawke and Uma Thurman had to abandon their eighteenth-century dream home in Sneden's Landing, New York, just after they had moved in, because of inexplicable incidents. It appears that they were too scared to describe what they had seen and experienced even after retreating to the safety of their old Manhattan apartment.

Rock star Sting was driven to call in professional ghostbusters when he discovered that his family were sharing their north London home with mischievous spirits. 'Ever since I moved there, people said things happened – they were lying in bed and people started talking to them, or things went missing. I was very sceptical until the night after my daughter Mickey was born. She was disturbed and I went to see her. Her room is full of mobiles and they were going berserk. I thought a window must be open, but they were all shut. I was terrified.' It seems exorcists did the trick as Sting and his kids now sleep soundly without unwanted interruption.

The late John Entwistle, bass player with The Who, enjoyed playing the role of the lord of the manor at his nineteenth-century country estate and was evidently prepared to share it with the previous resident. 'A lot of weird things have happened in the 22 years I've been here. Among them are sightings of a lady in nineteenth-century clothes walking the grounds, and the camera of an uninvited photographer falling apart. Most recently I was having trouble locating a recording of Keith Moon pounding out a never-used Who song, and so I asked my friendly ghost for a helping hand. A few hours later, when I was about to give up the search, the tapes spontaneously fell off a shelf behind me revealing the Moon recording which had been hidden behind them. I used it.'

One would think that living in a converted church would guarantee peace and quiet but Tim Robbins, star of the supernatural drama *Jacob's Ladder* and writer-director of the (ironically) titled *Dead Man Walking* was evicted from his home, a former chapel, by decidedly unholy spirits. 'It was in Los Angeles, 1984. I had just moved into a new apartment in a converted church. I had two cats. I came home one night – everything was still in boxes – it was dark and the cats were terrified. There were clearly spirits in the room. Then I looked on the wall and there were cockroaches all over it. I moved out the next day.'

John Lennon's widow Yoko Ono discovered a 'lost' Lennon song without supernatural assistance but when the surviving Beatles came to finish it they sensed the presence of the author overseeing the production. Paul McCartney and John Lennon were volatile soul mates and successful songwriting partners during the Beatles' heyday until their acrimonious split in 1970. So it is perhaps not unexpected that the surviving members sensed the late Lennon's presence in the studio when they reformed to record John's 'Free As A Bird' using his unfinished demo. McCartney has said, 'There were a lot of strange goings-on in the studio – noises that shouldn't have been there and equipment doing all manner of weird things. There was just an overall feeling that John was around.'

CELEBRITY SEANCE

Dave Grohl of rock band The Foo Fighters was sceptical when it came to the subject of the supernatural until his wife, Jennifer, persuaded him to join her in a séance. She had sensed unseen presences at their Seattle home and was determined to discover their cause. Grohl remembers, 'Jennifer asked if there were any spirits in the house. The glass on the Ouija board spelled out: "Y-E-S". I was just looking at Jennifer and she wasn't moving at all. The glass was travelling without her pushing it. Jennifer then asked, "What happened here?" The glass spelled out: "M-U-R-D-E-R-E-D". I asked who was murdered and got the reply: "M-Y-B-A-B-Y".' The couple has since learnt that according to a local legend, a native American baby was murdered there by its mother and buried in a well. The Grohls believe that it is her restless spirit which haunts their house grieving for the child and pleading with the present owners to give it a proper burial.

But it's not just Hollywood celebs and rock stars who admit to being spooked. Princess Stephanie of Monaco has confessed to having written a song with her dead mother, Princess Grace, who had died in a car accident in 1982. 'I found I'd written my own song and recorded it without really being present to the whole thing. Something was telling or guiding me to sit down and just write. I grabbed a pen and pad and the words came flowing out. I can't explain it, but I don't feel as if I wrote them. The words just came into my head as if someone on the other side was writing them down for me.' Her second album contained 'Words Upon The Wind', a song dedicated to her mother. According to her daughter, Princess Grace reappeared when Stephanie succumbed to stage fright during a French TV broadcast. 'Without my mother's help, I could never have done it. I was so petrified that I couldn't speak. Yet as soon as I got in front of the cameras, I could hear my mum telling me to relax and to just remember everything that she had always told me.'

CHAPTER 8

Ghost hunters

Fancy a spot of ghost-busting?
This chapter tells you all you need to
know, including a close look at serious
spook hunters' essential equipment.

S hortly before his death, ghost hunter Harry Price was asked to write an account of his most extraordinary encounter with the spirit world. The article, reproduced below, was published posthumously in the *Australian Herald* on Saturday, 3 April 1948:

HARRY PRICE — GHOST HUNTER

'Many times have I been asked for my "best ghost story": for the most thrilling and sensational incident in a lifetime's inquiry into the unknown and the unseen. I have investigated hundreds of alleged haunted houses, sometimes, as at Borley Rectory, with exciting results. I have attended thousands of séances, many of them in my own laboratory, in an attempt to pierce the "iron curtain" that separates this world from the next. I have sat in poltergeist-infested homes, in which objects have been flying about – objects which no human hands could possibly have propelled. I have seen crude limb-like materialisations form under my eyes when experimenting with the Schneider mediums. I have shivered as I watched the mercury fall during a séance, when normally the air should have become warmer. But only once have I seen what YOU would call a ghost – a solid three-dimensional spirit from, apparently, the other side of that "iron curtain" I have just mentioned.

'On November 8, 1937, a few days after I had broadcast a talk on haunted houses, a woman rang me up to tell an extraordinary story. She explained that she was the wife of a hop broker and had a large house in the South of London. Some years previously she had met a middle-aged widow who attended the same church. The widow, a French-woman, had been married to a British officer who was killed in 1916, leaving her with a young daughter, Rosalie.

'The widow determined to bring up her child in England, and made her home in London. The child, Rosalie, was never strong. In 1921, when she was six, she contracted diphtheria and after a few days' illness [she died]. The mother, whom I will call Madame Z. was heart-broken. She became ill with grief and nearly died. And then came the miracle.

'One night, early in 1925, when Madame Z. was lying awake in bed, she thought she heard her dead child's voice calling "Mother". She nearly swooned with fear and delight at the thought that her girl had "come back" and was still near her. She called her daughter by name but there was no reply. Next night and on many succeeding nights Madame Z. heard that same word "Mother" coming out of the darkness in the same loving, lisping voice that was so dear and so familiar to her. Gradually, she thought she could see in the dim obscurity of her bedroom the fluorescent outline of her child. She put her arm out of bed, she said, and her hand was clasped by that of Rosalie. After that, the visits became more frequent; the "spirit" more human, and mother and child even talked a little. That was the story told by the woman who rang me up. She added that in 1928 she persuaded Madame Z. to visit her home in order to see whether Rosalie could be induced to "appear".

'The experiments were successful and, in six months the child was materialising, regularly, in the home circle, every Wednesday night. I was invited to attend one of these séances. I was surprised when I was told that I could take charge of the séance, search the rooms, search the sitters, control anything and everything. The one condition was that I had to ask permission to do anything during the actual sitting, in order to avoid shock to Rosalie or her mother. This was reasonable. I accepted. The séance was fixed for December 15, 1937. After I had had supper with the family I began my search of the house, a large detached building. I examined every room. I sealed all external doors and windows. I removed most of the furniture from the séance room (the drawing room), examined the bare boards of the floor, sounded the distempered walls and ceiling, blocked up the chimney with newspapers, and finally sprinkled starch powder in front of the fireplace and locked door in order to register any possible foot or hand marks. Then I sealed the door and windows with adhesive tape and screw-eyes and drew the heavy curtains across the windows. A mouse could not have entered that room undetected. We were ready for the séance. It was 9.10 p.m. when I finished the job, watched – not without amusement – by the broker and his wife, his daughter, her boy friend, and Madame Z. With myself, these formed the sitters. I then searched them. No one was concealing anything. In the centre of the room I placed six heavy mahogany chairs in a circle. We sat down. My host switched off the lights. The séance began.

'Suddenly, Madame Z. gave a choking sob and murmured, "My darling!" I was warned that Rosalie was present. At the same moment I sensed that something was before me and that the distressed mother was fondling her child. Then something brushed my left hand; it felt soft and cool. I did not move, but asked permission to touch the figure. Permission was given, and I stretched out my arm, which came into contact with the nude and living body of a little girl, about three feet seven inches tall. I stroked her cheeks and rested my hand on her chest. I could feel her heart beating and could hear her breathing. Then with both hands I felt her hair, long and soft, falling over her shoulders. By this time most of the sitters were distressed.

'I got permission to examine the child be means of some luminous plates. I found that Rosalie was a well-formed little girl with dark, intelligent eyes, which gazed into mine without flinching. I received permission to speak to the figure. I hesitated, and finally said:

"Where do you live, Rosalie?" (No answer).

"What do you do there?" (No answer).

"Do you play with other children?" (No answer).

"Have you any toys there?" (No answer).

"Are there any animal pets?" (No answer).

'Rosalie simply stared, and did not seem to understand what I was saying. I asked her a final question: "Rosalie, do you love your mummy?" I saw her expression change and her eyes light up. "Yes," she lisped.

'Rosalie had barely uttered this single word when Madame Z. gave a cry and clasped her "daughter" to her breast. Our luminous plates were removed and the séance was over. Rosalie had gone. We sat for fifteen minutes, then the light was switched on. I found all my seals and controls intact. After thanking my hosts I left – not nearly as sceptical as I was a few hours before. I was impressed, puzzled, and almost convinced that survival of human personality had been demonstrated.

'I asked for another sitting, in my own laboratory, with a different group of observers. This was promised, but before it could be arranged Madame Z. went to visit her old home in Paris. This was at the end of August, 1939. She was apparently engulfed by the war and nothing has been heard of her since.'

MOST HAUNTED

Belief in ghosts and the paranormal has soared in recent years thanks largely to the success of the worldwide syndicated television series *Most Haunted*. The groundbreaking show which is avidly watched by millions in countries as far apart as Australia, Poland, Canada, Ukraine and Israel, investigates a wide variety of allegedly haunted sites in Britain and the USA using state-of-the-art audio visual equipment (including night-vision cameras) to record paranormal activity which lends the footage a *Blair Witch Project* feel. The show has attracted a cult following with fans getting together to hold *Most Haunted* parties when they draw the curtains, light candles and gather around the TV to share the shivers. The programme's website has recorded 30 million hits and 50,000 fans of all ages regularly apply for tickets whenever a live broadcast is announced.

The producers shrewdly assembled an investigative team of specialists from diverse disciplines to put their collective insights and experiences in perspective. Celebrity psychic Derek Acorah and psychic artist Brian Shepherd are complemented by historian Richard Felix and parapsychologist Dr Ciaran O'Keeffe. The idea is that if Derek psychically channels information of which Richard was previously unaware but is later able to confirm through research then it lends credibility to the claim that Derek made a genuine connection with the spirit world. Such an incident occurred at Sandbach Old Hall in Cheshire. Derek was adamant that he could 'see' Scottish soldiers fighting with swords at the site although Richard, who was an expert on the Jacobite rebellion, was equally adamant that Bonnie Prince Charlie's troops had not penetrated that far south. Subsequent research proved Derek correct. 1,500 soldiers under Lord George Murray had taken a detour to Sandbach to avoid clashing with the garrison at Manchester. As Richard said, 'If even I didn't know that at the time, how could Derek have known?' Derek's heightened sensitivity to the highly charged atmosphere and occasional 'possession' by the resident spirits must have convinced some of the most sceptical viewers of the existence of unseen presences.

Derek was a reluctant convert to mediumship even though he was just 'knee-high' when his grandmother overheard him talking to the ghost of his grandfather. Over the course of the next 30 years he developed a gift for psychometry (being able to 'read' impressions imprinted on personal objects by their previous owners), a talent he demonstrated to remarkable effect on an early TV series *The Antiques Ghost Show*. He attributes the uncanny accuracy of his 'readings' to his spirit guide 'Sam' who acts as intermediary between himself and the many disembodied intelligences who seek to communicate.

Psychic artist Brian Shepherd works in much the same way. When he arrives at a location he will walk around it until he feels drawn to a particular spot. Then he opens up to whatever presences may be near and lets his drawing implement glide across paper. He says when the connection is strong it is as if he is being guided. At first he has a sense of a person, then their features appear as if he is building an identikit from a given description. Invariably it's just a head, the rest of the figure being blurred. He chooses to work in charcoal because it is more immediate than colour, which he would have to think about and that would risk constricting the flow of images. At the Black Swan Inn at Devizes in Wiltshire he 'saw' a man with a bulbous nose sitting by the bar wearing a hat. When he showed the finished sketch to the landlady she burst into tears as she recognized him as the ghost she had been seeing over the years. Sometimes he appeared so solid that she has asked the bar staff why they haven't served him yet.

The locations for *Most Haunted* are kept secret from the psychics so that they cannot be accused of having researched the site prior to filming. In fact, the producers go to great lengths to ensure that Derek cannot be unduly influenced by knowing the location in advance. He is not given the name of his hotel until 24 hours before filming and that can be up to 45 minutes drive from the location.

There are more than 10,000 locations in the UK which have been officially registered and documented as sites of alleged hauntings and probably the same number again could have been registered, but for one reason or another their owners decided not to publicize the presence of their uninvited guests. One would imagine that such a large number of locations would mean that the production team would be spoilt for choice, but they have limited themselves to those claiming recent sightings which had been verified by several witnesses. Although it is primarily an entertainment programme, the *Most Haunted* team take the show very seriously and zealously guard their integrity. They go to enormous lengths to rule out physical causes for what might appear to be paranormal activity during filming. Before each show the technical team scours the site for electromagnetic anomalies using an EMF meter so that fluctuations during filming can be compared to the baseline measurement. Temperature readings are also taken which are compared with those made with a directional laser thermometer during the broadcast. Temperature changes are a positive indicator of a spectral presence. At Bodelwyddan Castle in Wales, for example, the presenter Yvette Fielding felt the spirit of her grandmother grasp her hand. The thermal-imaging camera showed Yvette's hands were blue while everyone else's hands were red.

The team also performs a lengthy and thorough walkthrough of the building to check for creaky floorboards, doors that might swing open with a draught, the noise level and vibrations caused by passing traffic or a railway line, loose pipes and even insect infestation. During their initial research they became aware that owners of commercial premises seemed suspiciously eager to discover that they might have resident ghosts as it makes for great publicity. In fact, they resisted a request from a major broadcaster to fake paranormal activity using special effects then admit what they had done at the end of the show. Their response was that even if nothing happened during filming it would still be riveting viewing to see how a paranormal investigation is conducted and to watch the team both in front and behind the cameras dealing with the 'scare factor'.

Surprisingly, it is the male members of the team who seem to be most sensitive to atmosphere. It's probably because they feel they have to laugh off the very idea of ghosts and so are unnerved when their preconceptions are shaken. Several crew members dropped out, including one of the big beefy riggers who ran the cabling, because they couldn't face their fears. 'They're all cocky when they arrive,' says Yvette, 'but at 2 am, when they have to de-rig in the pitch black, it's a different matter. I've seen huge guys walking hand in hand across a graveyard in the dark – it was quite sweet really.' Yvette herself is often torn between her desire for something uncanny to happen and her own fear of being spooked. 'I always say I want something to happen so we can capture it on camera – but when it does, I can't tell you how scared I am. Words can't describe it.'

The producers decided from the outset that watching Derek and the team sitting in hushed expectation in a single room would make for dull viewing so they only investigate locations where sightings have been made in at least three areas. Over the course of six series they have braved all-night vigils in damp underground tunnels, an isolated lighthouse, a prison, several treacherous towers, various ruined castles, country houses and windswept hillsides, all in pitch darkness and bitter cold.

And their verdict? Everyone involved, both in front of and behind the camera, admits to having seen or sensed inexplicable changes in atmosphere, to have heard strange unearthly sounds, to have smelt strong scents with no obvious source, to have been pushed, scratched and physically attacked by an unseen presence and to have been very, very scared indeed. The only contentious element is how they interpret their experiences. The team and crew are divided between those who blame spirits and those who suspect there might be another explanation such as an electromagnetic force field which scientists claim can cause headaches, auditory hallucinations and even the feeling of being watched in susceptible individuals.

Recently an ex-member of the group cast doubt on the validity of the evidence and the nature of the experiences shared by certain members of the team, but his colleagues have dismissed such claims out of hand.

IS YOUR HOUSE HAUNTED?

Have you ever sensed an invisible presence in your home as if someone was watching you, or perhaps seen something moving out of the corner of your eye? Maybe you've felt a touch like cobwebs on your face or a gentle pressure on your hair as if someone had laid an invisible hand on your head? Have you been kept awake at night by inexplicable sounds, smelt strange scents like perfume or tobacco, or perhaps you have a 'cold spot' in your house or flat which makes you uncomfortable when you approach it? If so, your home may be haunted, but there could also be a natural explanation for some of these anomalies and you need to be able to eliminate these before embarking on a paranormal investigation, as they can be expensive.

All houses are subject to 'settling' as the timbers in the roofing, joists and floors expand and contract with changes in temperature and these can cause creaks and groans that may be unsettling if you're a nervous and imaginative type. In very old buildings, rats and mice can be a source of scratching sounds, particularly at night when they scurry through the pipes, ventilation system and between the walls, foraging for food.

These are all obvious sources of unnerving sounds, but far less known is the fact that even such seemingly genuine sensations such as spectral caresses can be caused by fluctuations in your own energy field, or aura. Certain acutely sensitive individuals can be affected by the weather, particularly low pressure. Animals have an innate sense of an approaching storm or even rain as the atmospheric pressure changes under the gathering clouds. People can share this sensitivity but usually to a lesser degree and can become tired or develop headaches as a result. In extreme cases they may become depressed due to the change in pressure. Psychics can actually see an inverted funnel of mental energy pressing down on the head of a depressed person as their thoughts turn inwards instead of radiating outwards. For this reason, anyone who senses subtle pressure which they suspect may be caused by phantom fingers or the presence of spirits should first ask themselves if these sensations could originate within themselves. You can do this by relaxing into a light meditative state or trying automatic writing in which you can ask a direct question regarding the source of these sensations. Even 'cold spots' can have a rational explanation. Most houses have a spot where dampness can accumulate and this is to do with geological factors or the presence of an underground stream or pipes. A cold spot does not necessarily signify an evil presence, nor does a fall in air temperature which can trigger a fear response in the body. If you have eliminated all rational explanations and are keen to carry out a scientific investigation into possible paranormal activity, you will need to buy or hire certain items of equipment which no self-respecting ghost hunter can afford to be without.

The most essential item is an EMF meter which measures fluctuations in the electromagnetic field. Orthodox science considers these to be a natural phenomenon, but paranormal researchers believe these disturbances to be proof of the presence of ghosts. A normal EMF reading is between 0.5 and 1.5 milligauss so anything above this could be significant, especially if the reading fluctuates. It is important to be aware that domestic appliances such as fridges and microwaves and faulty wiring can cause unusually high readings.

If you still think you may have an uninvited presence in your home do not assume it to be malevolent. It is far more likely to be a loved one or friend who merely wants to assure you that they are well or to pass on information regarding your current circumstances or something they left unsaid. It is extremely rare to be plagued by a poltergeist (for which there is usually a rational explanation) or a spiteful spirit, so don't lose any sleep over it. If you suspect you have an unwanted presence, you can clear the property yourself or call in an experienced psychic who will exorcize it for you.

If you decide to do it yourself, you may find a spot of research at your local library to be useful in uncovering the history of the house and the area. Crimes, disasters and accidental deaths are usually recorded in the local paper or parish records. Maintain a detached attitude so that you are not unduly influenced by what you read. It is better to attempt communication first and then research the records to validate or dismiss what you have learnt from the spirit.

HOW TO SEE A GHOST

We are surrounded by spirits but unless you are acutely sensitive (psychic) you will be insensible to their presence. However, you can raise your awareness through meditation and exercises such as the one described over the page.

It is very important, though, that you protect yourself against mischievous and malevolent spirits as well as the strong possibility of self-deception, by grounding and centring yourself before attempting all psychic work, and remembering to close down at the end of each session. The exercise over the page will help you to achieve all these points.

Invoking Protection

- Stand with your arms by your side and establish a steady natural rhythm of breathing. With each in breath you will feel reinvigorated and with each exhalation you will dispel tension.

- When you feel suitably relaxed, visualize sending fibrous roots of etheric energy into the ground from the soles of your feet to anchor yourself. Then imagine a small sphere of white light hovering over your head.

Bring it down through the top of your head and see it pass through your body to the floor so that you now stand in a protective tube of light which radiates outwards dispelling the darkness and charging the air around you with divine energy. If you wish, you can invoke protection from whichever source you feel is right at this moment. 'The Lord's Prayer' would be suitable for a Christian, the invocation of the four archangels for the occultist. Do whatever feels right for you. You are now grounded and centred in yourself. Nothing can disturb you and nothing can invade your sacred space.

- If you live in an old house you can tune into the residual impressions of the previous residents using the following exercise. Otherwise you will need to find a suitable place such as an old church or hospital where you can sit for an hour or so in comparative peace.

- Keeping your eyes open, still your mind by focusing on your breath. Let your thoughts subside so that you settle into a passive state, receptive to the subtle impressions around you.

- Begin by making physical contact with the place. Stand with your back to a wall and take several deep breaths. If you are a natural medium you might be able to sense or see something straight away. If not, put your hands on something that will have absorbed an impression such as a chair, or church pew. Sit quietly. You may feel cold, heat or a tingling in your fingers. The atmosphere may also change in a subtle but significant way as you become sensitized.

- Next, heighten your sense of smell. If you are outdoors expand your awareness by centring on the scent of the grass, flowers and the soil. Hospitals will have their own distinct smells and churches too will have retained the smell of incense, flowers and polished wood.

- Now raise your awareness to the sounds that surround you and then see if you can go beyond those to the vibrations at higher frequencies. To do this, listen acutely to your watch or a clock. Home in on the ticking to the exclusion of everything else.

- Finally, soften your gaze so that any reflected light, such as through a stained glass window or off a polished surface, has a mildly hypnotic effect. Look beyond the light into the middle distance and see if you can detect a shape or figure. If not, look away into a dark corner and see if you can detect any movement in the shadows.

- If you are anxious for any reason, you can ask your inner guides or guardian angel to draw near, to isolate you from any disturbing influences in the atmosphere. You can help the process by stimulating your third eye. Simply make gentle, circular movements with your index finger in the centre of your forehead until you feel a tickling sensation. You are now open to the more subtle impressions in the atmosphere.

- Remember to close down and ground yourself when you have finished by counting down slowly from ten to one, stamping your feet and ritually rinsing your hands in cold water, anointing your face with cold water or discussing what you plan to do with the rest of the evening with your companions.

SPEAKING WITH SPIRITS

If we are surrounded by spirits – both malevolent and benign – how can we distinguish between those who wish us well and those who would do us harm? It is a popular misconception that spirits are summoned at the request of the medium and because of this many people still believe that spirit communication is wrong because it disturbs the peace of the departed. In fact, the reverse is true. Spirits come only when they have something that

363

they are desperate to impart to the living and they use a medium because most of us are not receptive to direct communication.

- For this exercise you will need a photograph of the deceased and, if possible, one of their personal possessions such as a watch or a ring. Take the photograph in one hand and the memento in the other. Make yourself comfortable, close your eyes and focus on your breath.

- Begin by drawing a circle of soft golden light around you to raise your awareness to a higher level and exclude any unwelcome influences. Now sensitize yourself to the residual vibrations in the personal object by centring your awareness in that hand. You should feel a warmth or a tingling sensation. If your psychic awareness is becoming more attuned you may even have a vision of the person you want to communicate with.

- If not, open your heart centre by imagining a small pulsating sphere of green light growing in intensity as you go into a deeper state of relaxation. Sense your heart centre softening and envisage the person you want to communicate with emerging from the light.

- If that person does not appear you may see your inner guide instead. If so, you can ask it to help you find the person you want to communicate with. Do not be surprised if they appear as they were when they were younger or in an idealized form as this is a projection of their self-image.

- However, you may not receive a visual communication. Instead you might have a sense of that person in the room, or hear their voice in your inner ear. If it is a lady you may have a scent of their perfume. If it is a man who smoked you may become aware of the smell of their favourite tobacco.

When you are ready to return to waking consciousness close down, clear the aura and ground yourself using the techniques previously described.

THE GHOST HUNTER'S TOOL KIT

You don't need expensive equipment if you're starting out as an amateur ghost hunter. Initially all you need is a digital camera or a 35mm autofocus camera with flash, loaded with 400 ASA film for interior shots and 800 ASA film for exterior work. Although 35mm film is now technically redundant, serious paranormal researchers and certain professionals such as forensic photographers still use it because the images are more difficult to manipulate than digital and therefore less likely to have their authenticity questioned. However, digital cameras have one major advantage. Their memory cards offer a far larger photo capacity than film (for example an 8Mb memory card can store over one hundred pictures) and the unwanted shots can be erased and the card reused. Digital enables you to take dozens of pictures in sequence without worrying that you are using up valuable film. When you want something more serious you might consider a motion sensor scouting model mounted on a tripod which takes a series of pictures automatically when the sensor is triggered. But make sure it is fitted with infrared bulbs so that you can shoot in the dark.

Ghosts don't generally pose for pictures so although a succession of still shots will capture the trail of a moving spirit, a camcorder would be more practical. Again, ensure the model you choose has an infrared nightshot feature for recording without a light source rather than a night-vision scope which has serious drawbacks, including the risk it poses to the user when flash guns are in use. When choosing a camcorder don't forget to budget for an infrared light extender which increases the camcorder's night vision range from 10–100 ft.

For the audio aspect (such as electronic voice phenomena) choose a digital DAT recorder with an external multi-directional microphone. A cassette recorder will create too much mechanical noise and its dynamic range is extremely limited. When it's quiet you won't hear much above the hiss and motor hum. An external microphone minimizes the amount of machine noise picked up by the mike and is of infinitely superior quality. If you invest in a digital recorder with a voice activation feature you won't have to spool through hours of silence to locate the recording you want.

An essential piece of equipment is the electromagnetic field detector which measures fluctuations in the electromagnetic field. Models vary in sensitivity and range from 3–25 ft depending on the price. Most have either an LED or audible alarm to notify the user that they have a reading. This can be helpful if you are working mostly in the dark. Commercial contact thermometers can be useful in measuring cold spots. Alternatively, remote thermometers can scan several rooms at the same time while you monitor them from a central location.

Motion detectors are absolutely essential and

surprisingly inexpensive. They produce an audible signal whenever an infrared beam is broken. You may also want to consider non-essential items such as walkie-talkies, and heavy duty torches (with a red filter to reduce glare), plus notebooks to record EMF, temperature readings and details of where and when the photos or camcorder footage was taken. It is easy to forget where and what was taken in all the excitement and this will devalue your evidence. And, finally, don't forget to pack lots of spare batteries as ghosts have a knack of draining power, so leaving you literally in the dark.

HOW TO CONDUCT A GHOST HUNT

You can conduct a ghost hunt in your own home or at a suitable site such as an old church, theatre, public house or battlefield. Remember, if you are investigating a site that is not your own home or on public land you will need to ask the owner's permission. Ghost hunts are best conducted by a small group who can verify each other's findings. Also, it is much more fun to work with others. If you work on your own there will be no one to verify your findings and act as a witness and if you fall in the dark there will be no one to call on for help.

Choosing A Location

Graveyards are to be avoided. Ghosts tend to linger in locations where they lived or where they died and rarely where their body is buried. They do not associate themselves with their physical shell and many believe they are still alive.

Graveyards can also induce a morbid turn of mind in those who are sensitive to atmosphere and it is necessary for serious investigators to maintain an objective, scientific approach. On a purely practical level, graveyards tend to generate a confusion of residual energies due to the number of bodies buried there over the centuries and these energies can also be mixed with those who have mourned their passing. It is better to choose a location where you are likely to pick up isolated individual impressions and where there is a minimal risk of being overwhelmed by paranormal activity and discarnate entities.

Invoking Protection

It is strongly advisable to begin every investigation with a prayer or invocation for protection whether you are religiously observant or not. Such rituals serve to ground and centre you so that you will not be easily disturbed by experiences which may or may not have a supernatural origin. You can imagine drawing a circle of white light around you and/or invoking protection from the four archangels, a religious figure or your spirit guides. Take what you are doing seriously and show respect for the dead otherwise you risk a psychic attack – one you cannot see and whose strength and nature you cannot determine.

If it is an interior location you will need to conduct a thorough preliminary walk through in daylight to establish EMF and temperature baselines. You will need to take readings near domestic appliances so that you are not fooled by any abnormal readings in these areas during the actual investigation. Although it may seem obvious, it is surprising how many ghost hunters forget in their eagerness to check for loose latches on doors and windows and for draughts which can cause creaking doors or chill winds. You will also have to take practical steps such as noting where there are steps or other potential hazards so that you don't stumble over them in the dark.

Remember also to take sample photos of the area in good light so that you can identify where significant readings, sightings and sounds took place. When all of these precautions and preliminary checks have been completed, it is recommended that you bait a spirit trap with a personal object associated with the history of the individual in a sealed room. Choose a room that has seen activity in the past, or is most likely to register activity. The object can be placed on a sheet of plain paper and an outline drawn around it so that it will be seen if it is moved by unseen hands. Alternatively, you could place the object on a dusting of flour or talcum powder so that you can rule out a draught which would disperse the flour or a cat which would leave paw prints. Then mount a lock-off camera with a motion sensor on a tripod and point it at the object. If you want to guarantee no one will tamper with the experiment you can set up a separate motion detector as an alarm then seal the room from the outside with tape. You can now explore the rest of the site with a camcorder, still camera, EMF and temperature equipment leaving the locked room until last.

When you are finished, it is important that you close down by asking for the blessing of the divine on the location, on those spirits which linger there and on all those involved in the investigation. Thank the angels, or spirit guides whose presence you invoked at the beginning and then ground yourself by drinking cold water, rinsing your hands and talking aloud about what you plan to do with the rest of the evening or the next day. Do not be tempted to begin analyzing the data, but start fresh the next day. This will ensure you view the material with detachment and that you do not carry a residue of emotional energy from the site.

Afterword

The aim of this book has been to demonstrate that ghosts are not the malevolent entities of horror fiction and folklore, but the manifestation of a wide range of natural phenomena including residual personal energy, projections of our etheric essence, surges of kinetic energy (which account for most poltergeist activity) and discarnate spirits. Such phenomena have occurred across the centuries and appear to be common to all cultures. They serve to reinforce the widely held belief that death is not the end but merely a transition from one state of being to another. However, our material existence appears more real because it involves interaction with matter in a denser three-dimensional world where change can be measured in time and movement by distance, so giving the illusion that we exist at a fixed point in time and space.

The cases included in this book, specifically those involving bilocation and those in which individuals have assumed an idealized form after death or during an out of-body experience, suggest that this illusion of solidity and finality is a creation of the brain whose perception and understanding is determined by its physical limitations and processing power. Under certain conditions, our True Self, which appears to be pure consciousness or mental energy, can transcend the physical dimension to glimpse a greater reality which mystics have known of for millennia. This is a reality which millions of ordinary people have experienced during their encounters with the paranormal, although science is only now beginning to acknowledge it following the development of quantum physics. Unfortunately, paranormal experiences have frequently unnerved many people because they were unprepared to have their perception of life and death challenged in such a dramatic fashion. Ghosts, it appears, only instil fear in those who do not believe in their existence. Those who stubbornly refuse even to consider the possibility of life after death are fast becoming the modern equivalent of those who once asserted that the Earth is flat.

I have been aware of the presence of spirits for many years and find them reassuring rather than unsettling. I have often sat writing at my computer and felt what can best be described as cobwebs brushing my cheek, a soft hand stroking my hair or insubstantial fingers pressed gently on my chest or back. When I was younger, the thought of being aware of the presence of ghosts would have unnerved me, but having studied various esoteric techniques and having practised meditation over many years I have lost my irrational and unfounded fear of the unknown. However, I remain acutely aware of the dangers of dabbling in spurious activities such as Ouija boards or conducting séances.

My own experiences have taught me that the more

we understand our true nature, our world and its non-physical counterpart – the world of spirit – the less fearful and apprehensive we become. As children we believe that our world will exist untainted by change, that our friends will be with us always, that our parents will live forever and that adulthood and death is as far from our world as the stars in the night sky. But as we grow older we are confronted by the inevitable process of change and come to acknowledge our own mortality. For those who deny the existence of an afterlife and dismiss the paranormal as irrational, the universe is no more than a marvellous mechanism and while existence is to be endured or enjoyed it has no more significance than a passing storm. The existence of spirits reveals that this belief is erroneous and it severely limits our understanding of the nature of the universe and our part in its unfolding.

Life and death are not mysteries but they are hidden from us because we choose to deny the evidence that surrounds us in the cycle of the seasons, the regenerative power of nature, the succession of night and day and the cyclical processes of science in which nothing is destroyed, only transformed.

Bibliography

Atwater, P.M.H., *Coming Back to Life* (Ballantine 1991)

Barrett, W., *Death-Bed Visions* (Methuen 1926)

Crookall, Robert, *The Supreme Adventure* (James Clarke & Co 1961)

Currie, Ian, *Visions of Immortality* (Element 1998)

Edward, John, *One Last Time* (Penguin Puttnam 2000)

Holroyd, S., *Mysteries of the Inner Self* (Aldus 1978)

Jung, C.G., *Memories, Dreams, Reflections* (Vintage Books 1961)

Kraalingen, Elleke Van, *Beyond the Boundary of Life and Death* (Publisher unknown)

Moody, R.A., *The Light Beyond* (Rider 2005)

Moody, R.A., *Life After Life* (Mockingbird Books 1975)

Monroe, R.A., *Journeys Out of the Body* (Doubleday 1971)

Morse, Melvin, *Closer to the Light* (Ivy Books 1991)

Muldoon, Sylvan, *The Phenomena of Astral Projection* (Rider 1987)

Muldoon, S., *The Case for Astral Projection* (Aries Press 1936)

Myers, F.W.H., *Human Personality and its Survival of Bodily Death* (Longmans, Green 1903)

Osis, K. and Haraldsson, E., *At the Hour of Death* (Hastings House 1977)

Praagh, James Van, *Talking to Heaven* (Signet 1999)

Richelieu, Peter, *A Soul's Journey* (HarperCollins 1996)

Rinpoche, Sogyal, *The Tibetan Book of Living and Dying* (Rider 2002)

Ring, Kenneth, *Life at Death* (Quill 1982)

Ring, Kenneth, *Lessons from the Light* (Moment Point Press 2000)

Roland, Paul, *Explore Your Past Lives* (Godsfield/Hamlyn 2005)

Roland, Paul, *Investigating the Unexplained* (Piatkus 2000)

Wheeler, David R., *Journey To The Other Side* (Grosser and Dunlop 1976)

Wilson, Colin, *Afterlife* (Caxton Editions 1985)

Zaleski, Carol, *Otherworld Journeys* (Oxford University Press 1988)

Zammit, Victor, 'A Lawyer Presents A Case For The Afterlife' Various editors, *Mysteries of The Unknown* (Time Life)